CRYSTAL HEALING:

2012 AND BEYOND

DISCOVERING AND USING ROCKS, CRYSTALS AND STONES IN THE NEW AGE

Barbara S. Delozier, Msc.D.

BALBOA.
PRESS

A DIVISION OF HAY HOUSE

Balboa Press books may be ordered through booksellers or by contacting:

Balboa Press
A Division of Hay House
1663 Liberty Drive
Bloomington, IN 47403
www.balboapress.com
1-(877) 407-4847

Because of the dynamic nature of the Internet, any web addresses or links contained in this book may have changed since publication and may no longer be valid. The views expressed in this work are solely those of the author and do not necessarily reflect the views of the publisher, and the publisher hereby disclaims any responsibility for them.

The author of this book does not dispense medical advice or prescribe the use of any technique as a form of treatment for physical, emotional, or medical problems without the advice of a physician, either directly or indirectly. The intent of the author is only to offer information of a general nature to help you in your quest for emotional and spiritual well-being. In the event you use any of the information in this book for yourself, which is your constitutional right, the author and the publisher assume no responsibility for your actions.

Any people depicted in stock imagery provided by Thinkstock are models, and such images are being used for illustrative purposes only.
Certain stock imagery © Thinkstock.

ISBN: 978-1-4525-3292-9 (sc)
ISBN: 978-1-4525-3294-3 (hc)
ISBN: 978-1-4525-3293-6 (e)

Library of Congress Control Number: 2011902788

Printed in the United States of America

Balboa Press rev. date: 3/9/2011

DEDICATION

To you, the reader and crystal practitioner, may you always Trust the Process of Life and look to the Spirit of Nature to guide you.

To you, my family and friends, thank you for supporting me in all my ventures. You are the greatest blessing!

And, to Laurence Hargrave late of New Age Stones ~ thank you 'Larry Coyote' for opening up the globe to me through your awesome knowledge and worldwide contacts for rocks, crystals and stones.

EPIGRAPH

"Crystals are sentient. Each crystal holds within itself an energy that can communicate with us, as do rocks, stones, driftwood, seas-shells, and coral. Life lives within them, so please respect them as living entities. Rocks, crystals and stones can heal, help and make our lives more livable in a most basic way ~ all we need to do is 'listen' to what they have to say.

Crystal may tell you "place me next to your water bottle before you drink the water." Doing so will energize your drink. Crystal may tell you to place it next to your food, or place it in your bath, or ask to go for a ride with you. When Crystal speaks, listen closely and enjoy a communication like you have never known before!

I like to breathe into my crystals and stones. I do this by holding them up to my mouth when I speak to them. This is a personal and intimate way to communicate with crystals, rocks and stones. I also like to hold a crystal to my brow energy center to feel its personal energy when I greet one; rocks and stones seem to like this type of greeting as well. Try it!"

With warmest crystal blessings in Love, Light and Sound always,

Bee ♥

ENDORSEMENTS

"In this life, Barbara has been fascinated with a conscious life-form as much a part of Mother Earth as our physical bodies... the Stone People. In the process of following her interest in these Stone People, she has learned many of their secrets, their talents and of the gifts they have to share with humanity. In Crystal Healing: 2012 And Beyond, Barbara shares with us much of what she has learned in the decades since her youth. There is much wisdom in this book for those who have the open eyes to see truth, the open mind to learn truth and the open heart to know truth." ~ Dhyana Markley, Author, and owner of http://AscendedMastersSpeak.com

"Bee Delozier offers a beautifully written, clear and definitive guide to help readers understand and connect deeply with the healing potential of crystals and gemstones. Drawing on her personal experiences from her decades-long fascination with the mineral kingdom, she expertly illustrates how developing a relationship with stones can lead us into a greater awareness of healing ourselves and the planet. This book is a valuable resource for any library." ~ Carole J. Obley ~ author I'm Still with You ~ http://SoulVisions.net

"I just had the privilege of reading the advance copy of "Crystal Healing: 2012 and Beyond." When she was at our crystals mine, Barbara told me her plans to write this book. I was anxious then for her to get it published. Barbara has the guidance, the wisdom and the knowledge of an inner clarity that will help, strengthen and empower you. Her words always help me to stay focused; she teaches with spiritual knowledge. Plus, I have a hard time ending our conversation.. Like trying to put the book down.. excellent, Barbara." Becky Young, Sweet Surrender Crystal Mine, http://sweetsurrendercrystals.com

CONTENTS

PREFACE

I trust that the power and energy that exists between me and the rocks and stones that I have befriended are the same power and energy given to us from the Creator Source. This is the power of nature, and it exists within All Living Things. We are all a part of this energy, we live in it, and it flows in and around us — rocks, trees, pets, wildlife, people, fish, birds — and no matter where we live on Mother Earth, we are connected.

Learning to listen to rocks, crystals and stones is not a difficult step to take; all it requires is an open heart and an open mind.

With us moving closer and closer to 2012 and beyond, rocks, crystals and stones are soon to take their rightful place within the order of things on Mother Earth. Our forefathers knew of their wisdom and used it to heal themselves and to communicate. We, too, can use this same energy in our now.

The energies of rocks, stones and crystals are increasing and some are changing altogether. There is not much written about the change, but it is being given to any number of light and energy workers who are sharing this information in the best ways they can. I am only one of many who have chosen to hear what the stones have to say.

Stones are more powerful than we think, we cannot hurt them by dropping, chipping or cracking them. When a stone, rock or crystal chips or cracks, it is a form of communication that the stone is 'opening up' for us. Rough edges, chips and cracks in a stone or crystal add to the rocks' character and experience. Often, these stones are considered 'empathic', meaning they have experienced pain and so, can help us to overcome pain in our own lives. Much the same way we have 'smiley' lines on our faces, so do rocks, stones and crystals have their own 'smiley lines'.

Don't be afraid to speak with your rocks and crystals. Ask them to speak to you. Ask them to be your friend. Thank them for being in your life, and thank God for creating them, as well.

2012 ushers in a time of change, a time when bringing in the new is assisted by new thought, new age, and new attitudes. 2012 heralds the ushering in of personal, spiritual and planetary changes that will benefit all life forms on Planet Earth and within the multi-universes upward through the Spiritual planes.

Every day, we are discovering new and useful ways to utilize tools from Mother Earth, communicate with her children, and each other. *Crystal Healing: 2012 and Beyond* was created with the intent of improving that communication between nature and humanity.

As a youngster, I always remember talking to rocks and stones, picking them up, fondling them, putting them in my pockets. My folks just wrote it off as a little girl's tomboy attitude, wanting to play with dirt, rocks and stones, but for me, it felt like something more. As I grew, so did my collection of rocks and stones, some of which I've carried with me for years and years. The fascination never ended, only improved over time as I began to realize that these little Earth gems held their own power, their own consciousness and if I listened …. they had a lot to say.

The intent of this book is to help you understand more about the powers of rocks, crystals and stones, and how these energies are changing to suit the good of the whole in the New Age. I hope you find the information contained in this book useful and that it is accepted with pure intent for yourself and for those whose lives you touch.

With warmest blessings of the purest frequency in Love, Light and Sound always,

Rev. Bee
Barbara S. Delozier, Msc.D.

ACKNOWLEDGMENTS

Randy Skates and Becky Young, Sweet Surrender Crystal Mine, Sims, Arkansas ~ http://SweetSurrenderCrystals.com

Jim and Kathy Fecho, Fiddlers Ridge Rock Shop and Bear Mountain Crystal Mine, Mt. Ida, Arkansas ~ http://fiddlersridgecrystals.com

Julie and Dennis Kincaid, Crystal Seen Trading Co., Mt. Ida, Arkansas ~ http://crystalseen.com

Laurence Hargrave, New Age Stones ~~ http://newagestones.com. Larry transitioned from the physical plane on April 19, 2010, but his legacy of knowledge and love of the use of rocks and crystals continues to live on through this book and many crystal practitioners. Thank you, Larry Coyote.

Tyberon – James Tipton, the Earth Keeper organization ~ http://earth-keeper.com.

INTRODUCTION

Rocks, crystals and stones are advancing in use for 2012 and beyond. The powers and energies of crystals, rocks and stones have been changing over these past few years. Their intent has grown stronger and they are touching into many different areas where they have not touched before.

Crystal books that were written prior to 2008 may not have current information because specific meanings and activities attributed to crystals, rocks and stones have increased in vibration and frequencies in accordance with Earth Changes. Some frequencies may change altogether as we approach the Age of Aquarius, what is considered the Golden or New Age.

Energy workers who frequently use crystals, rocks and stones are being prepared for these changes, often in dream state, and sometimes through physical connections with other energy workers. Many energy workers are being downloaded with new and novel uses for stones and crystals. I say this out of my own, personal experiences and have been given accelerated use for many objects that we consider 'inanimate' such as sea shells, driftwood, minerals, gems, rocks, stones and crystals.

The information contained in this book has been gleaned from years of my own research, my personal experience and from downloaded information from my guides, Ascended Masters, and Angels who have been patiently working with me for many, many years. I am very grateful for this guidance.

I have been very fortunate to have worked with and met many crystal and stone practitioners, some of who are mine owners and others who are simply appreciators that love the look and feel of rocks, stones and crystals. No matter what term is used to describe a person who works with stones, each and every person is in their own way a facilitator.

The best advice I can offer you as a facilitator is to stay connected with your crystals, rocks and stones so that you, too, may feel changes in vibratory rates and frequencies of them. If you are feeling changes, please make note and share your experiences with others. Let's all share the information that we are receiving in the NOW as we move closer to transitional change.

2012 ushers in a time of change, a time when bringing in the new is assisted by new thought, new age, and new attitudes. 2012 heralds the ushering in of personal, spiritual and planetary changes that will benefit all life forms on Planet Earth and within the multi-universes upward through the Spiritual planes.

PINEAL GLAND ACTIVATION IN THE NEW AGE

The pineal gland is connected to both the crown chakra and brow chakra (third eye or Tisra T'il). Crown chakra and third eye (Tisra T'il) activations are occurring with increasing frequency in those of us who are conscious of the connection. Those who are not conscious of the pineal and third eye activations will become more so as the frequencies increase. We are evolving into multidimensional BE-ings of love, light and sound through the activation of the piezoelectric impulses generated by rocks, stones and crystals, and in particular, the calcite crystals within our bodies. The pineal gland, located at the top of the brain stem deep inside the brain, serves as our own individual crystal repository and acts as a receiver of information transmuted to us through light and sound.

The pineal gland vibrates at a high frequency, resonating at 936 Hz. It emits the musical note B with a violet-white color. Amethyst, charoite, dumortierite and lepidolite radiate the pineal gland frequency, as does quartz crystal, Herkimer diamond, selenite and some of the human-enhanced aura crystals. These stones and frequencies can be used to open and activate the pineal gland.

The pineal gland is known to be the seat of Christ Consciousness which by the way does not have to do with Christianity; rather, it deals with the very high level of energy emanating from Soul in the inner worlds. Pineal gland activation raises our consciousness to the higher self and allows visualized utilization of universal life force energies.

Each of us, through the pineal gland, is a vortex that empowers and magnetizes us to our personal ascension and that of a group consciousness, linking us directly to the universal mind collective.

French philosopher Renee Descartes believed that as we see with two eyes (light) and hear with two ears (sound), so must we join two into one at the center of Soul, the pineal gland. The pineal gland is thought to carry the whole of Soul and to unify what is seen with the eyes and heard with the ears to form visions through the Tisra T'il, or third eye.

Within the pineal gland and the inner ear are large numbers of micro-crystals of calcite. These calcite micro-crystals are charged with piezoelectricity, which fine-tunes our vibratory and frequency rates. Have you ever wondered why you are drawn to one person and not another? More than likely, your vibratory and frequency rates resonate with the person to whom you are attracted. The attraction is electrical, which is also why we sometimes get that spark of excitement that is felt physically when we meet someone who vibrates at our same rate.

Stimulating the pineal gland affects you physically, spiritually, and psychically. You can stimulate the pineal gland to help with its activation in various ways, although one of the best ways to strengthen it is by the use of crystals and stones.

For as long as I can remember I would sense if something was right for me by placing it up to my third eye chakra. If something was right for me, the sensation at my brow chakra would feel good, warm and fuzzy. If something was not right for me, the sensation felt cool, cold and unfriendly. I didn't know it back then but what I was doing was using the connection from the tisra t'il to the pineal gland to access extrasensory perception and make an assisted choice. We can stimulate the pineal gland by holding certain crystals and stones to the tisra t'il.

Amethyst can be placed over the brow chakra during meditation or chakra balancing exercises. While lying down, place an amethyst to the tisra t'il and then go into meditation in your usual way. The frequency and vibration of the amethyst opens the third eye chakra and the quantum pathway to the pineal gland, irradiating it with intense healing violet light. Charoite, sugilite, purple fluorite, lepidolite, alexandrite, and iolite are all wonderful activators and can be used in a grid around the head during meditation.

Place a blessed stone or crystal etherically on the third eye energy center and visualize its energy aligning the brow chakra to the pineal gland. Instruct the etheric stone to remain in action for the duration of your meditation period.

Massage essential oils into the brow chakra and the hollow at the base of the skull to clear and cleanse the pineal gateway. Helpful essential oils are frankincense, myrhh, sandalwood, and cedar; use one drop. If an oil is too strong for your skin, mix one drop with a half teaspoon of carrier oil such as sweet oil, almond oil or grape seed oil.

Diffuse essential oil in an oil burner or mist diffuser.

Chanting helps to activate the pineal gateway and the pineal gland itself. The words OM, AH and HU all carry their own individual signature frequency and when chanted for periods of up to 15 minutes a day, act as regulators and activators for the pineal gland.

Listening to solfeggio harmonics at 936 Hz opens up the pineal gateway and greatly enhances the ability to transcend the physical plane during meditation. If you are not familiar with solfeggio frequencies, they are the original music scale as used by monks in the ancient Gregorian and Tibetan chants. Sound healing the body, mind and spirit, as well as pineal gland activation is supported by the use of solfeggio harmonics.

Although there are a number of places to discover solfeggio frequencies online - a quick search will prove fruitful – my favorite spot is SourceVibrations.com.

Since the new millennium, we have been increasingly moving forward toward higher vibrations and frequencies in preparation of our personal ascension, our group consciousness ascension, and ascension as a planetary unit. These vibratory and frequency activations have been heralded by the passage of the Triple Gateway portal dates.

TRIPLE GATEWAY PORTAL DATES AND ASCENSION

Time as we know it is accelerating more and more quickly as we approach December 12, 2012, also known as 12.12.12, the last of the triple gateway portal dates in the 21st century. Every living thing on Planet Earth is being affected by these triple gateway or portal dates, including plants, animals, and minerals. When these dates pass, time will continue to accelerate, but at a much higher frequency. We are awakening to meet and greet the New Age and our frequencies are expanding to fill the vacuum created by the rising conscious awareness.

The first New Age portal opened on January 1, 2001, or 1.1.1 which marked the beginning of the new millennium in spiritual terms. Many light and energy workers felt the powerful energies rise from the crystalline grid on Planet Earth that heralded the opening of the star gate from the Seven Sisters Star System. This date also reawakened the sleeping potential of light and energy workers and they began to recognize their place within the metaphysical porridge. 1.1.1 acted as a validation for those who had already stepped upon the journey of love and light, and an initiation for those awakening Souls .

On February 2, 2002, or 2.2.2, the grid stepped up its power again incrementally, increasing psychic abilities, intuition and extra sensory perception in those light and energy workers who were willing to take up their tasks. "Willing" is the operative word here because although many were being called, not all were willing or able to hear.

The sequential date of March 3, 2003, or 3.3.3 again brought in another power up of energies through the triangulation created by the triple portal date. Assisted by the star system Sirius B, the gateway activated Universal blessings for higher purpose and established a deeper connection to the Universal Consciousness. To many of us, 333 has a special meaning ~ to me, it is a time when my consciousness reaches its highest point during the day or night and acts like a balance to the ebb and flow of my personal biorhythm. Often, I wake up to find 3:33 on the clock next to the bed and have also experienced interdimensional contact around this time in the early morning.

On April 4, 2004, or 4.4.4, we as a collective began to see our dreams turn into reality as the creative energies began to swell and form a wave of incredible power up from the crystal repositories around the globe, fueling a more active dream state for light and energy workers. The numbers 444 have a deep, spiritual meaning.

Darlene Virtue in her book *Angel Numbers* describes 444 as a sign that "thousands of angels surround you at this moment, loving and supporting you…" The numbers 444 in sequence tell us that we are protected, loved and guided from a higher source so it only stands to reason that 4.4.4 as a gateway portal creates an energy essence of receivership for blessings from the creative multi-verse.

Continuing through the sequential dates leading up to 2012, May 5, 2005, or 5.5.5, gave us an increase in our spiritual abilities that pulled forward and manifested positive change, improved our flexibility and adaptability with freedom of movement through the dimensions. More light and energy workers came on board, increasing a pronounced energetic creative reaction, heightening the brilliance of the Light interdimensionally. The date 5.5.5 corresponds with the fifth plane of God, the Soul plane, and opened up a direct conduit between the physical plane and the Soul plane. Many light and energy workers felt the significant increase in Christ Consciousness energies, which 555 accentuates in the physical.

On June 6, 2006, 6.6.6, the Masters and High Level Spiritual Guides established more balance, harmony and diplomacy from a spiritual level on Planet Earth between the factions of Light and Dark, causing an inward drift on the continuum through the dimensions. More and more light and energy workers came online using their gifts in accordance with their spiritual heritage – Lemurians and Atlanteans, working together. The sequential date of 6.6.6 brought forward the positive/negative frequency of 3D, the third density of the physical world, shedding a brilliant light on the power of love. 6.6.6 corresponds with the sixth density or spiritual plane that is a focus of magnificent effort.

On July 7, 2007, or 7.7.7, a strong power up from the Pleiades (Seven Sisters Star System) connected with Andromedan, Sirius B and Arcturian energies to promote a pulse of esoteric magic focused on vibratory frequencies. I feel blessed to have experienced part of this powerful energetic axis at Gilliland's Ranch in Washington State on 7.7.7 with a spectacular sighting and visitation by a beneficent Being of Light. Once more, light and energy workers across the globe felt the surge and stepped up to take their place within the grid.

On August 8, 2008, or 8.8.8, the sacred Atlantean Blue Crystal of Knowledge in Arkansas powered up … activating the energies of infinity, positive repetition and success throughout the grid system. Yes … more light and energy workers stepped up to accept their roles and participate in the process of preparing for Ascension globally.

This Blue Crystal of Knowledge activated the First or Blue Ray, cutting away negativity and allowing the essence of crystalline knowledge to enter our atmosphere.

September 9, 2009, or 9.9.9, we experienced activation of four of the Atlantean power crystal repositories bringing the energies of completion, resolution, and forming a bridge over the gap to bring about a better world with genuine love, peace, and clarity.

The Emerald Crystal of Healing activated on 9.9.9 which in turn increased the energies that reprogram both the Emerald (or 5th) Ray and Platinum (or 4th)Ray . The 5th Ray is the green ray of healing and truth and the 4th ray is the white ray of purity and harmony. Healers were given the strength to become better healers, teachers were given the wisdom to become better teachers and seekers of wisdom were given the gift of greater insight. Balance and harmony is now further supported through these powerful activations.

In Brazil, another Atlantean crystal repository, the Gold Crystal of Healing Regeneration activated on 9.9.9. Along with the Gold Crystal of Healing Regeneration, the Sixth or Gold Ray activated, which is the ray of Peace and Harmony bringing with it a firmer foundation for balance and harmony.

Deep within Mt. Shasta in California, the Om Crystal of Multidimensionality activated on 9.9.9 which brings out the reprogramming and alignment of the crystalline energy between humanity and the planet.

Every living thing on Planet Earth contains crystalline particles, trace elements and minerals in perfect balance and harmonics. These will all reprogram into alignment with the triangulation between Planet Earth and the core central between the four star systems in the heavens – Sirius B, Andromeda, the Pleiades and Arcturia, in preparation for Ascension. The very fiber of our bodies will re-ignite with DNA modifications.

Many of us have already begun to feel stretching in the areas of our chakra energy centers. Although this process may physically feel uncomfortable, there is no reason to feel fear. The healing energies of rocks, crystals and stones will help us acclimate to these physical changes.

On October 10, 2010, or 10.10.10, the Violet Crystal of Sound in Bahia Brazil activated. This Atlantean crystal is associated with Saint Germain and the 7th or Violet ray. It is a high frequency spiritual energy that transmutes negativity or anything negative lodged within our spirit and expels it through the use of sound waves and harmonious vibration. 10.10.10 tells us that it is time to take action, physically, emotionally, mentally and spiritually.

On November 11, 2011, or 11.11.11, the Platinum Crystal of Communication in Arkansas will activate heralding the year of revelation and oneness. This is a most powerful activation date being that the number 11 is a master number. Seeing the date as month, day and year it equals 33, the highest of all master numbers, which possesses a powerful potential for change. The triple portal date of 11.11.11 will bring with it a shift in the dynamics of our world, the way we perceive it and our abilities to comprehend the dramatic changes as positive and pure. The master number 33 represents the master teacher, and brings our focus toward the spiritual upliftment of all mankind.

The number 33 also stands for the double triangle, hexagonal star, or merkaba, that which contains the soul body. See *Violet Flame of Count Saint Germain Merkaba*.

Yes, we walk the thin razor's edge with this triple master number by acknowledging the power to create great fear and anxiety, or the purest love and stability. We choose our own experience. My knowing is that determination, trust and love will carry us forward from 11.11.11 and on into the New Age of Aquarius in wisdom, light and sound vibrations of purest intent.

December 12, 2012, or 12.12.12 which is nine days before the Winter Solstice 2012, marks the end of the Mayan calendar. In the hearts and minds of many, this date ushers in the Age of Aquarius, the Golden or New Age and with it, the full activation of sacred Crystalline energies across the entire grid, the way-shower for Ascension. Deep within the Bimini bank in the Bahamas lies the Ruby Fire Crystal of Energy, which will come on line and power up on 12.12.12. The Crystal of Thoth in Tiahuanaco, Boliva also activates on this date, bringing all nine Atlantean crystals on line in an incredibly powerful surge of high-end energy.

Arkansas is by far the largest of the crystal repositories on Planet Earth, with the highest quality of brilliance, hardness, and electrical energy of all the world's crystals, rivaling those in Brazil, Tibet and Madagascar. These crystals were seeded by the Power of One from Atlantis at the time shortly before its fall, where they created an Atlantean community.

Further research has uncovered the metaphysical connection between Lake Titicaca in Bolivia and Crater Lake, in Oregon. While Lake Titicaca is home to one of the Atlantean crystalline powerplant activators at Tiahuanaco, Crater Lake is the only repository for a volcanic feldspar crystal, a stone formed in molten lava. Known today as Oregon Sunstones, these beautiful crystals are highly charged with crystalline energies and are regarded as gem grade, making them a highly sought after stone. Oregon Sunstones are most often found in the high desert of Lake and Harney counties, where they were deposited after being expelled into the air through volcanic eruption of Mount Mazama thousands of years ago.

Oregon Sunstones were affected by the 9.9.9 activation through the connection to Lake Titicaca and the Sun-Moon Crystal of Light, the Atlantean powerplant crystal in Bolivia. If you have Oregon Sunstones … good for you ! Hold them near and dear to your heart and allow their activated energies to permeate your being-ness! They bring clarity, honesty and an empowerment of pure intention to those who befriend them. These beautiful stones will emerge in 2012 and beyond as a viable source of spiritual renewal and healing for mind, body and spirit.

HEALING 2012 AND BEYOND

The year is 2025. You are scheduled for a delicate surgery involving the movement and repair of an inner organ. Your doctors tell you that your surgery is scheduled for 9 am and that your release time will be 10 am whereupon you will walk out of the surgery center ready to resume normalcy in your life. Imagine that your delicate surgery will be performed by a skilled crystal surgeon who will make precision surgical cuts by use of a crystal wand, rather than an invasive scalpel. Her cuts will be created with an activated Quartz crystal wand that will create and seal the wound as it works – all without touching you.

A crystal practitioner will be on board to fortify and support your body during and after the surgical procedure with the use of different stones, crystals and minerals placed in a grid around your body. Before you leave the surgical center, the practitioner places etheric stone implants within you which he programs to work for 72 hours. After the programmed time passes, the etheric implants will disappear, leaving no trace other than the feeling of well being and pleasant energetic sensations.

Delicate and intricate treatments will be effected through the use of minerals, stones and crystals.

Stone grids will be used much like we use them today, to keep someone or something within the protective shield of crystal energy ~~ except that the energies are amping up daily, increasing in strength.

The above is the scenario for the use of rocks, crystals, stones and minerals in the upcoming Golden Age, 2012 and thereafter. This is not science fiction. This is our reality for the New Age.

Remedies and elixirs will take center stage in our healing process. These practitioner tools will be delivered to us via distance healing, riding the wave of energy from healer to recipient, and will be created personally and individually for our specific needs.

Doctors, nurses and medical practitioners will stand side by side with crystal practitioners in unity working for the good of the whole. Each will have their place in the scheme of things to help humanity and no one's abilities will be ridiculed. Utopia you think ? Science Fiction perhaps? No, not at all .. this, too, is our reality in the New Age.

NEW AGE BIRTHSTONES
BY MONTH AND SUN SIGN

Most of us are familiar with stones by the gem that is associated with the date of our birth. Wearing a birthstone is thought to bring good luck and good health to the wearer. The recognized list of birthstones changed from the biblical, or traditional birthstone meaning, to the modern day birthstone meaning sometime around the early 1900s promoted by the gem industry. Today, although we recognize both the traditional and the modern day meanings, here is a third option for the New Age ~ birthstones for 2012 and beyond.

Month	Traditional	Modern Day	New Age
January	Garnet	Garnet	Granite and Azeztulite
February	Amethyst	Amethyst	Phenacite
March	Bloodstone	Aquamarine	Aventurine
April	Diamond	Diamond	Sugilite
May	Emerald	Emerald	Dioptase
June	Alexandrite	Pearl and Moonstone	Lepidolite
July	Ruby	Ruby	Kyanite

August	Sardonyx	Peridot	Malachite
September	Sapphire	Sapphire	Chrysocolla
October	Tourmaline	Opal and Tourmaline	Amazonite
November	Citrine	Yellow Topaz and Citrine	Rhodochrosite
December	Zircon	Blue Topaz and Turquoise	Lapis Lazuli

Astrology also plays a role in the choosing of a birthstone. Some of us may resonate with the astrological birthstone rather than the month designation. The following are Sun Sign birthstones as given to me in meditation for 2012 and beyond. Some of these stones may be new to you; however, many new rocks and stones are coming into activation at this time.

Being a Scorpio sun sign myself, I found it interesting that Tiger Iron is my new astrological stone because it has become a favorite of mine recently. It is a powerful stone, beautiful to look at with a deep, dark side in between the bands of golden and red crystallization. When I looked at the stone, I realized that my Higher Self was spot on with Tiger Iron as a resonating stone for the Scorpio sun sign because it holds within the mysteries that are inherent in the Scorpio personality.

I also suggest that as a secondary support stone, you consider your Moon and Rising signs as well. For instance, I am a Scorpio with Pisces Moon and Pisces Rising; my astrological power stones are Tiger Iron and Charoite. I hope you find the below information helpful for you in discovering your personal astrological birthstones.

Sign	Dates	Color	Element	Stone
Aquarius	Jan 21 – Feb 19	Sky Blue	Air	Apatite
Pisces	Feb 20 – Mar 20	Lavender	Water	Charoite
Aries	Mar 21 – Apr 20	Red	Fire	Carnelian
Taurus	Apr 21 – May 21	Green	Earth	Chrysoberyl
Gemini	May 22 – Jun 21	Yellow	Air	Yellow Jasper
Cancer	Jun 22 – Jul 22	Silver	Water	Moonstone
Leo	Jul 23 – Aug 21	Gold	Fire	Tiger's Eye
Virgo	Aug 22 – Sep 23	Lt. Green	Earth	Atlantisite
Libra	Sept 24 – Oct 23	Pink	Air	Rhodonite
Scorpio	Oct 23 – Nov 22	Maroon	Water	Tiger Iron
Sagittarius	Nov 23 – Dec 22	Purple	Fire	Lepidolite
Capricorn	Dec 23 – Jan 20	Brown	Earth	Combarbalita

HISTORY AND FOLKLORE

Romans, Egyptians, Native Americans, indigenous people around the world for eons have considered minerals and gems to be of spiritual value.

Color was prime importance. Seers and oracles used auric colors and meanings and put them toward gem colors with similar spiritual meaning. Clear or white for purity, clarity; blue for spirituality, spiritual connection; red for passion, love; yellow for honesty, loyalty; green for healing; pink for unconditional love and so on.

The Egyptians valued gold, sliver and copper, and mined for gold and copper. Silver was imported as a trade item. They also mined for malachite, emeralds, carnelian, amethyst and turquoise. Excavation pits in modern Egypt date back some 40,000 years, showing that even Middle Paleolithic Egyptians placed value on these minerals and gems.

There is evidence that early Native Americans used quartz for arrowheads, knife blades and ceremonies in areas where quartz crystal is prevalent ~ Arizona, Arkansas, New Mexico, Georgia, and numerous other areas across the United States.

Native Americans mined copper, lead, iron, turquoise, amethyst, gold, silver and other gems and minerals for trade and for their own use. Volcanic glass, known as Obsidian, was a rare but welcomed commodity for early Natives because it made the best sharp edges for tools and weapons. Native American artisans also used Obsidian for ornamentation.

Aborigines used shells, coral, ivory, amber and minerals for medicinal and spiritual use. Pre-Columbian indigenous peoples in Florida used shells, coral, and medicinal clays for healing, as well.

Indigenous people of North America understood the concept that all things ~ tangible and intangible ~ had a vibration, and they used these vibrations to help them choose what they needed and for what purposes. Often, the medicine man or woman would be in charge of tuning in to the vibratory rate of others including mineral and vegetable, although all could recognize the feel, it was the medicine person who was responsible for interpreting the meaning and putting it to use for the good of the whole.

The medicine person or healer would often read rock and stone formations as signs from a higher deity and interpret these signs as messages. Even today, rocks and stones communicate with us. Have you ever been strongly compelled to pick up a particular rock, stone, shell or piece of driftwood? This happens when an inanimate object wishes to communicate with us. They work very hard to raise the height of their energy field, causing their vibratory rate to grow outwardly so that we will notice them. This is how rocks and stones communicate with us to offer their wisdom and to give us ample opportunity to work in concert with them. As our forefathers used this knowledge, so may we today.

The Mayan culture relied on the use of rocks, crystals and stones in their sacred, healing and creative lives. Mayan structures were built of stone; stone masonry and artistry was a large part of their culture. Numerous excavations at ancient Mayan sites have uncovered pieces of rock crystal that suggest that crystal was often used in their rituals, for curing their ills, as well as for divining. The power of crystals was believed to be the Mayan's connection to Earth and was particularly powerful.

It has long been known that the Aztecs used crystal and stone in their weaponry but they also used crystal as a tool of divination. Crystal skulls have been discovered throughout Mexico, Central America and South America. Such discoveries allege that these 'Skulls of Death' were used by Aztec and Mayan shamans to produce death of an enemy.

The Maoi of Easter Island are huge stone monoliths, carved figure-heads, that dot the coastline of the island which were carved from local stone. History shows that some of these huge stone carvings aligned with the stars and moon, once again, making an example of the use of rocks and stones as metaphysical tools.

The Egyptians were a dualistic society of miners and excavators who were very progressive for their time. Gem stones were used to adorn their clothing and as artisan work for royalty. The knowledge and use of gold by the ancient Egyptians rivals that which we know today. Healing with crystals and stones was widespread during ancient Egypt and stones were known for their powers of protection.

In fact, ancient civilizations worldwide were well versed in the use of crystals, rocks and stones for healing, divination and prophecy. The symbiotic energy between man and the Earth was part of the magical connection that resulted in crushed powders, elixirs, jewelry, and use in rituals and sacred ceremonies.

Whether the rocks, crystals or stones were used rough or cut and polished into gemstones depended upon the intention of the user, similarly to how we use stones today. However, our use of rocks, crystals, stones, shells and Nature's healers is reverting back to the ancient ways, far and beyond what we now know as we usher in the New Age, 2012 and Beyond.

GEOPHYSICAL PROPERTIES OF CRYSTALS AND STONES

Color, luster, transparency, twinning, fracture, hardness, fluorescence, refraction, cat's eye effect (chatoyancy), striation, magnetism, odor, feel, taste, solubility, piezoelectric properties, thermal properties and radioactive properties are some of the geophysical aspects of minerals – crystals and stones.

The first thing that we notice with stones or crystals is their color or lack thereof. Next, we usually notice luster and texture. Luster is the shine or brilliance of the color. Texture is how the stone or crystal feels outwardly, if it is rough, smooth, or angled.

Tumbled stones are smooth, having have the roughness worn away by a grinding medium in a tumbler, or otherwise are cut and polished. Raw stones and crystals may have matrix attached, matrix being the fine grained mass in which the crystals or stones are embedded.

Rough gemstones, rocks and crystals are considered natural, working stones. Their energies have not been altered in any way, and any irregularities, chips, cracks or broken spots are thought to contain the most potent form and amount of healing energy.

Often, tumbled and polished stones are used as touch-stones and are much easier to carry in your pocket or purse without snagging. The energy of a tumbled stone is focused and centered.

Jewelry made from rocks, crystals and stones retains the same vital energy as the rough or tumbled versions of the stone, and also has the added energies of the precious metal used in its design.

Rocks, crystals and stones are made of minerals. Some stones are made from a combination of minerals, such as Boji™ Stones, Puddingstone, Atlantisite, certain Fuschite, etc. All minerals are classified into eight groups, such as:

Native Elements – copper, silver, gold, nickel-iron, graphite, diamond

Sulfides – spahlerite, chalcopyrite, galena, pyrite

Halides – halite, fluorite

Oxides and Hydroxides – corundum, hematite

Nitrates, Carbonates, Borates – calcite, dolomote, malachite

Sulfates, Chromates, Molybdates, Tungstates – celestite, barite, gypsum

Phosphates, Arsenates, Vanadates – apatite, turquoise

Silicates – quartz, almandine garnet, topaz, jadeite, talc, biotite mica

The shape of the stone is determined by the chemicals at the location where the rock or stone formed; these chemicals become a part of the mineral, and also the stone. Large hunks of mineral-laden rock are called massive minerals; however, where there is a definitive shape comprised of flat sides, the rock or stone is called a crystal.

Crystals were formed millions of years ago when the liquefied rock from within Earth's core worked its way up through to the Earth's crust – then cooled. Some of the liquefied rock found its way into cracks and crevices of other rocks. Some crystals were formed by the action of rain, filtering down through volcanic ash and sediment after an eruption. Whole forests of trees are 'petrified' in this manner, the wood pulp being crystallized through compression. Northeast Arizona is home to both the Petrified Forest and the Crystal Forest caused from an enormous volcanic eruption some 200 million years ago.

There are three types of rock – metamorphic, sedimentary and igneous. Metamorphic rock is rock that has been changed by the rock cycle – weather, erosion and compaction. Sedimentary rock has been formed by compression. The cooling and subsequent hardening of magma forms igneous rock.

Examples of sedimentary rock are breccia, limestone, gypsum, sandstone and shale. Examples of metamorphic rock are quartzite, marble, schist, slate, and gneiss. Examples of igneous rock are andesite, basalt, dacite, pumice, rhyolite and obsidian.

Be aware that some rocks and stones, as beautiful as they may be, might also contain toxins that are dangerous. Many stones contain traces of heavy metals, such as copper, arsenic, lead, antimony, sulphur, iron and mercury. When creating a gemstone elixir, gem water or charged massage oil, do not add the stone physically to your mixture if it contains any metal. Rather it is preferable to use an indirect method. I have added cautions to stones in this guide where necessary. Some stones are so toxic that they should only be handled with protective gloves, such as Cinnabar and Realgar.

A good rule of thumb is to avoid any rock or stone that is shiny or metallic-like in your drinking water, elixirs and massage oils. If a rock or stone has a metallic shine, the chances are good that it contains metal and metals are toxic. Other colors to avoid in your drinking or gem water, gemstone elixirs and massage oils are bright blue and green indicating traces of copper, also toxic.

For blessing your drinking water, creating elixirs and massage oils, you might consider using etheric stones, rather than physical ones, particularly if the stone is mined along with copper, silver, lead or other metal. Quartz crystal is not toxic ~~ although the acids used to clean them certainly are toxic.

TYPES OF CRYSTALS AND STONES

Crystals and stones come in many different shapes, colors, sizes and types. The following information provides descriptions of different types of rocks, crystals and stones you may find.

Acicular – An aggregate of long, thin crystals that are needle-shaped and form a net-like growth. An example of acicular crystal is Natrolite, belonging to the Zeolite family of minerals.

Aggregate - Grouping of crystals of one or more mineral types which are clustered in a dense mass. Agate is a good example; as is Puddingstone and Granite.

Arborescent - Cluster bearing structural resemblance to the branching qualities of trees. Gold and Silver are good examples.

Bladed - Flat crystals shaped like blades of grass or knives. Kyanite is an excellent example of bladed crystallization.

Blocky – Crystals that have a boxy appearance with flat sides. Selenite sometimes has this crystallization habit.

Cubic -- Crystals that have a point on each corner, forming a cube.

Dendritic – Crystals that contain inclusions that resemble plant like patterns.

Dodecahedron -- A crystal that has ten faces.

Double Terminated Crystals – Crystals that have balance with points at each end. Some are self-healed double terms and some are formed this way in nature. Herkimer Diamonds and Tibetan Quartz are good examples.

Druse - Outwardly oriented crystals that look like the inside of a geode. Amethyst and Quartz crystal are good examples.

Equant - rounded, angular crystals with three nearly equal perpendicular axis. Fluorite is an excellent example.

Fibrous - An aggregate of fine, typically parallel, thin, thread-like crystals.

Fracture – Refers to the appearance of a newly chipped, or broken surface forming an uneven face. Quartz often contains fractures.

Geode - Outer shell of one mineral that encases a layer comprised of a different mineral. Example: Amethyst cathedral within an aggregate shell. Volcanic in origin.

Hexagonal - A crystal that has six faces.

Octahedron – A crystal that has eight faces. Fluorite is a good example.

Opaque - Solid coloration of crystal, usually white or light gray in which light does not penetrate.

Orthorhombic -- Crystal with a double pyramid shape that forms a rhombic prism.

Phantomed - Crystals that stop growing for a while, then resume growth forming smaller crystals within that are 'trapped'. The phantom has the shape of the crystal of when it stopped growing.

Sceptered - Crystals that stop growing for a period of time, then resume growth but only on the upper part, not the lower portion.

Tabular - Crystals, also referred to as 'Tabbies' that are thick and flat, sometimes with opposing side being wider than the other.

Tetrahedron – The tetrahedron is one kind of pyramid which is a polyhedron with a flat polygon base and triangular faces connecting the base to a common point.

CRYSTAL FORMATIONS AND METAPHYSICAL MEANING

Abundance Crystal – numerous small crystals growing out around the base of larger crystal. Brings abundance of energy and enhances state of abundance. Additional properties in 2012 and beyond bring spiritual prosperity and accelerated growth for user.

Barnacle – smaller, delicate crystals attached to the sides and/or faces of a larger crystal. Helpful with family or group issues. Brings harmony and trust to groups. In 2012 and beyond, Barnacle crystals will also bring blessings of the sea, returning the user to their water roots in spirit. Protection from drowning and removes fear of water.

Bridge / Inner Child / Penetrator Crystal -- has a separate crystal protruding partly or fully from a larger crystal. Considered to be spiritual bridge between inner and outer worlds, as well as a bridge between oneself and others. Good for public speakers. Enhances spiritual growth. Good for spiritual teachers. In 2012 and beyond, Bridge/Penetrator crystals' properties enhance to permit user entry into higher dimensional wisdom temple for learning and instruction.

Candle Crystal / Atlantean Love Star / Pineapple Quartz -- numerous smaller terminations surrounding a larger central point. Contains gentle but powerful energies. Works with the heart chakra energy center to soothe and open blockages. Lightworker and Energyworker stone. Contains ancient Atlantean knowledge. Used in meditation to access ancient wisdom. 2012 enhancements offer opportunities for user to visit crystal sources on the inner planes for teaching direct from Atlantean and Lemurian Masters.

Cathedral Crystal (Castle crystal) -- has a castle or cathedral-like shape with spire-like terminations – uplifting energies of balance; relieves depression and anxiety. Used to access Akashic Records and travel to wisdom temples. Wonderful tool for those who are called to minister to the spiritual needs of others.

Channeling Crystal – (7-3 Crystal) -- has a 7 facet face on the front with a triangular face directly behind it. Helps to access truth and wisdom. Helps channelers to stay balanced so they can make the connection to the Higher collective. 2012 and beyond offers further enhancements and empowerments to those who possess a 7-3 crystal, and more 7-3 crystals will find their way into the hands of those who can operate with them.

Cross Crystal – Appearance wise, this crystal shape resembles a Penetrator or Bridge Crystal, yet power-wise, it is very different. This is a stone of powerful healing energy that pulls in the Christ Consciousness, to heal, soothe and clear the pathway to higher sense of Godliness and true spiritual up-link to the Divine. It is a wonderful stone for relationships because it heals the rifts that surface when two try to become one. The two crystals "cross" each other, but remain separate and whole as individuals, yet, are joined in unity which promotes deeper understanding and ability to merge ideally without limiting the other's growth. It is a good meditation crystal because it lifts one up to the Higher Realms with grace and peace.

As a talisman, these crystals are used to facilitate daily efforts to accept differences with loved one and promote peace in a family unit of strong wills. Some folks consider these crystals to be "X" crystals, representing male integrity, bringing the male energies to balance.

Crystal Cluster -- Crystals that have grown in a group or cluster that are sometimes intertwined and/or branched out. This is a harmony crystal that enhances group energy. Wonderful tool for those who work with group consciousness and whose work brings them before the masses. 2012 enhancements offer the user improved and intensified powers to work with the higher collective in unifying and bridging residual differences that separate us dimensionally.

Curved or Bent Crystal -- crystal with a natural curve to its shape. Considered to bring flexibility to those who are inflexible in perception and attitudes. Good tool to help you make decisions.

Dolphin Crystal (Mother and Child crystal) – larger crystal with a smaller one that seems to be riding along side it, like a mother and baby dolphin swimming together. This is a protective crystal that projects nurturing, love, and parental energies. Metaphysical stone that brings spiritual growth.

2012 enhancements augment and realign the energy centers of the user to facilitate access to the ancient wisdom of the Nommos and the use of sound as a healing tool. Crystal has been and will continue to be used to channel sound, and the Dolphin Crystal is one of the many tools being made available to us for this purpose.

Doorway Crystal (rectangular)– has rectangular-shaped face (like a door). Mystically and logically enhanced crystal. Use by meditating/contemplating on the doorway to enter the ether worlds in meditation. Ask a question and the answer will come through meditation. Good for asking questions before meditating on the doorway. An answer is received by traveling through the doorway into the higher planes. Ask for guidance and it is received. Rectangle doorways are logical receptors.

Doorway Crystal (diamond shaped) -- mystically and creatively enhanced crystal useful for artists and those who use their creativity. Use by meditating and /or contemplating on the doorway to enter the ether worlds in meditation. Ask a question and the answer will come through meditation. Good for asking questions before meditating on the doorway. An answer is received by traveling through the doorway into the higher planes. Ask for guidance and it is received. Diamond shaped doorways are creative receptors.

Double Terminated -- crystal with points on both ends. These are the energy movers .. they transmit and receive; good for soul travel, healing, dream work and meditation. Double Terminated crystals grow alone, usually in a clay source and are not attached to matrix. These are wonderful stones for strength of purpose and decision making. Also excellent stones for someone who is undertaking a solo endeavor, or striking out on their own. Double terminated crystals are often found in Tibetan quartz and Herkimer Diamonds.

Dow Crystals (Trans-channelers) – Discovered by Jane Ann Dow, a natural channel and divinatory, a Dow Crystal has three 7 sided faces separated on each side by a triangular face. The crystal point makes a 7-3-7-3-7-3 configuration. This is both a transmitter and channeler crystal. This is the perfect balancing tool, also an excellent healer on all planes, physical, emotional, spiritual, mental

– enhances creativity and service to humanity with spiritual and mystical energies.

Elestial Crystal (Skeletal) -- layer upon layer of natural terminations over the face of the crystal that resemble steps or etched layers. These are the calming crystals, the calmers and soothers of the mineral world. Used to uncover hidden secrets. Helps to detoxify the internal organs.

2012 empowerments bring Elestial crystals on board to heal skin conditions, rashes, and will be used to remove internal parasites from the body by drawing them out and away from the internal organs.

Empathic Crystals (Warriors) – crystal that has been damaged, scratched, or with chunks missing from the tip and/or sides. These crystals have been through their own war and came through it, so they now are here to help us get through our own personal wars. Teaches empathy for the pain of others and brings the knowledge that true beauty comes from within. Compassion, healing and teaching crystal.

Enhydro Crystal – crystal with water bubbles inside – these are relationship crystals and help with reducing stress. This is a very powerful crystal because in most cases the water that is contained in the bubbles is hundreds of thousands of years old. Sometimes, the fluid within the bubble may be an oily residue from carbon, plant or animal, but most often is ancient waters. The most powerful Enhydro Crystals show movement of the water bubble. This is a great crystal for connecting to past lives or ancient time. Good to help clear up karmic relationships. 2012 enhancements to encourage time travel both forward and backward, if the user desires so in meditative state.

Etched Crystals -- natural etching on the sides or inside the crystal. Used for mystical connection or contact, particularly with lost civilizations – Egypt, Atlantis, Lemuria, Mu, Telos and so forth. Contains healing information and techniques. Excellent for meditation and for personal development. Psychic's crystal.

Extraterrestrial Crystal (ET's) -- single point at the top with multiple small points growing downward at the bottom forming a rocket-like appearance.. Assist in connecting to star friends, especially helpful to star children and those associated with knowledge of UFOs and ETs. Powerful crystal to connect with guides and angels, too. Helps to amplify confidence level and courage. UFO

Experiencers ~ abductees and contactees ~ will particularly enjoy the feeling of protection afforded by Extraterrestrial Crystals.

Faden Crystal (FAH-den) -- threads of fluid or gas is visible on the inside of the crystal that look like a milky or feathery line. Sometimes called a 'fibrous' crystal. Great attunement crystals, good for soul and dream travel and to 'feel' alternate dimensions. Faden Crystals are considered to be growth crystals that help us to activate a new pattern of growth, transition smoothly to a new path.

Fairy Frost (Devic) Crystals -- visible wisps, veils and fractures that make it appear that the inside of the crystal is frosty. Devic crystals hold mystical energies in that they can communicate with the elementals, nature spirits. Learn to communicate with fairies and elementals by using a Devic crystal. Tell your crystal that you wish to learn to communicate with nature and .. then, listen closely. This crystal has the ability to open hearts and promote universal love of all beings. Wonderful tool for Celtic Reiki practitioners, masters and teachers. Also works very well for those connected to the elementals.

Family Cluster – two parent crystals with one or more smaller 'child' crystals around it. Promote harmony of family life in groups. New 2012 enhancements bring this crystal more on board as collective crystal with a sound frequency emanating above 528 hz. Immediate uplink to sound vibration and frequency for those working with toning and raising the vibratory rate of the Universal collective mind.

Gateway Crystals – Similar to Key Crystals, a Gateway crystal has an opening into the interior of the stone. This opening is deeper and more pronounced than a Keyhole. Gateway Crystals are used to enter dimensions and planes where one might not normally be admitted without earning entrance. However, with permission, the user can gain access to deeper understanding, finer information and innermost discoveries.

Generator Crystal (Merlin Crystal) -- has six equal faces terminating in a pyramid point at the tip. Generates energy and magnifies your purpose. Stimulating to the chakra energy centers, this crystal will clear blockages and remove negativity of all types from the aura. Also used as a group crystal, meaning it connects those in a group creating unity between members.

Grounding Crystal – has an eight-sided face somewhere on the crystal. Very unusual growth and a rare find, this crystal aids in keeping the psyche in check, dispelling the feelings of being lost or unconnected to reality.

Growth Crater Crystal – formation is similar in appearance to a *keyhole* indentation but is four sided rather than three sided. Growth craters are caused naturally when one crystal separates from another. Symbolically, growth crater crystals help the user to stand in their own power, discover their own realization and strike out on their own with confidence. Excellent tool to help relieve one of habits that no longer suit, but continue to hold on. Use growth crater crystal during meditation and ask to see the point in your life where you 'found' the habit, so you can correct the pattern from that point on. This is a 'new beginnings' crystal.

Included Crystal -- Crystal with minerals inside. These are crystals that enhance our inner qualities and help us to discover our inner selves.

Isis Crystal - has a face with 5 sides. This crystal is connected to the Divine Feminine energy and is an excellent crystal for women to use. Promotes creativity, wisdom and loyalty. Also helps men connect with their feminine side.

Keyhole Crystal -- Crystal has either a 3 sided indentation or a 6 sided indentation that looks like steps leading into the crystal. Wonderful for discovering hidden meaning or secrets. Problem solver, helps to find answers to serious questions. Keyhole crystals also lead the way to Self-realization when used as a meditative tool.

Laser Wand – long, thin crystal with small faces on the point. These crystals help to focus energy with surgical precision. Excellent tools for psychic surgery. Laser wands are sometimes called 'singing wands' because of the beautiful sound they create when rubbed or rolled together. When you tap a singing laser wand to another singing laser wand, they produce a tinkling sound that opens doors to the higher planes, aiding in meditation and contemplation. As with all wands, be careful where you point it! This is a powerful tool, particularly when energy is charged up through our emotions. Helps to break up stagnant energy masses, clears up blockages and helps to reshape energy fields. Excellent for meditation. Very powerful vibration and frequency, these crystals connect the user directly to the Divine by direct link up.

Left Activation Crystal/ Right Activation Crystal – has an inclined window to the left or right of the front (largest facet). Left Activation crystals are a Time link to the past said to increase left brain, while Right Activation Crystals are a time link to the future and said to increase right brain function.

Lemurian Seed Crystal -- has a matte finish and patina, with horizontal striations on the sides. Seeded tens of thousands of years ago by the ancients and set to activate in the Age of Aquarius. Programmed with a conscious connection to unconditional love and acceptance of equality and spiritual teachings. Wonderful for dream work and interpretation.

Lineated Crystal- has parallel indented lines or raised lines along the sides. Improve work areas and used for vision quests, spiritual journeys, divination, intuitive knowledge. Excellent for diabetics and those who suffer from blood disorders. Improves eyesight and helps with Parkinson's disease. Eases pain of child birth.

Manifestation Crystal – A crystal within a crystal, a manifestation crystal helps with bringing your desires into reality. Removal of blocked painful memories.

Needle Crystal – long, narrow and slender crystals. Delicate with a very high vibration. Good for healing. See *laser wands*.

Phantom Crystal – crystal appears to have the outline of a second crystal inside. A phantom crystal is an awareness tool. Good for metaphysicians, channelers, psychics, mystics and spiritual seekers.

Rainbow Crystal – fractures inside give the appearance of prismatic rainbows within the crystal. Helpful for drawing out negativity , these crystals can lighten a heavy mood. Good for grief counselors, and personal consultants who deal with the negativity of others. Rainbow Crystals are believed to be the closest manifestation of pure white light energy that can be witnessed on the physical plane. Use Rainbow Crystals during meditation to reach into the realm of Light Energy for healings, knowings and manifestations of your wishes as suits the good of the whole.

Record Keeper Crystal – has a raised or etched triangle on the face or side of the crystal. These are spiritual stones because they hold information within that is released to the holder through meditation.

Scepter Crystal -- symbol of power, to be used wisely. Very powerful manifesting crystal that empowers the user to obtain that which is desired. Make certain that what you wish for is what you really want, or need, because this crystal will bring it. Scepter crystal also empowers user to forgive themselves and others for transgressions, real or imagined. Aligned with the heart chakra energy center. Recognized by second crystal growth on top, mushroom-shaped and symbolizes male power and energy.

Self-Healed Crystal – easily recognized by a healed break where a broken termination is healed over by a druzy formation or pattern. Some self-healers completely grow back or form into double terminations over time. Wonderful tools to heal childhood trauma of neglect, abuse and abandonment.

Shovel Crystal – has one face that is elongated like a shovel. Working crystals that help you to discover the right solution for a current problem without guesswork. Good for self-work because it helps you to dig to the bottom of the matter.

Sigil Crystals -- often referred to as "Sacred Sigils," you can recognize a Sigil crystal by the oddly shaped etchings on the face that represent symbols that have meaning to you. Sigils are highly personalized crystals that call out to whomever it is that resonates at the same vibration. When holding a crystal, you might notice etchings that resemble things, such as a mountain, or a stream, a lightning bolt, a geometric shape such as square, triangle, rectangle, or circle, which shape is repeated over and over again on the face. By recognizing the symbols you can begin to discover what the 'Sigil' means for the particular crystal and … what it means for you.

For instance, a square may represent the Earth, connected to the four points, north, south, east and west. A circle may symbolize the Universe, encompassing the All That Is; a lightning bolt may represent a messenger meant to make an impact statement from above; a triangle may represent Divine presence; a mountain may represent powerful Earth energies; and a stream may represent cleansing, healing energies. A crystal that contains squares, circles, triangles, lightning bolts, a mountain and a stream on its face in a repeated fashion may be telling the user that they are connected with the energies of the Earth, Universe, and the Divine in healing, cleansing and helping others, as well as themselves, to stand up, take notice of change and be empowered for the good of the whole.

Sacred Sigil Crystals are being discovered in our NOW, more so than ever before, as we move closer toward 2012 and beyond, and never before has such power worked its magic outwardly to the masses where it is now being received by so many people. This is indeed a blessing and *Sacred Sigil Crystals* are one of the most wonderful blessings of the New Age.

Singing Wand Crystals – see *Laser wands*

Soul Mate Crystal – usually two gas or fluid bubbles side by side that refract rainbow colors when held in the light. Psychically charged crystal that blesses the holder with deepening love and spiritual attachment in a relationship. Helps to work through karma quickly and effortlessly with a significant other.

Sugar Crystal - This crystal appears to have been rolled in sugar, with granular 'sugar' crystals attached to the face and sides. Harmony, beauty and positivity are the qualities of a sugar crystal.

Super Seven Crystal - crystal that displays St. Elmo's Fire within that resembles the aurora borealis. This stone has the energies of amethyst, Clear Quartz, Smoky Quartz, Rutile, Goethite, Lepidocrosite and Cacoxenite. Also known as "Melody's Stone," it is one of the most potent crystals to have activated. Promotes the new while helping to disperse the old. Helps with healing and ascension. This is a stone for the New Age and 2012 enhancements from the Triple Gateway Portal Dates, especially in Brazil in 12.12.12, will furnish this crystal with high powered energy pulses that will erase negative energies, heal past life karma and remove engrams from both the physical and emotional body.

Tabular Crystal – flat crystal, sometimes rounded and sometimes square or rectangular. Tabbies can store information and can be used to activate and clear other crystals.

Time Line Crystals – Time lines are rectangular windows just below and adjoining the main face of the crystal. They either point left or right. Left Time Line Windows reach into the past, while Right Time Line Windows reach toward the future. Both are considered to be access points when used in meditation to retrieve information as needed from the past or the future.

Transmitter Crystal – 7-3-7 crystal – two 7 sided faces with a triangle face between them. Help to connect to higher self and higher wisdom.

Trigger Crystal – has small crystal protruding out of one side shaped like a trigger of a gun. By gently squeezing the 'trigger', this crystal is activated to give you a burst of strength, endurance and mental acuity. Also, when aimed at other crystals, it helps to strengthen their attributes..

Twin Crystal – Sometimes called Soul Mate crystals, a Twin Crystal has two separate and defined crystals growing side by side that often share a common base. Also known as relationship crystals, said to help keep relationships going smoothly. Good for like minded individuals to find their way; it teaches valuable life lessons that All life is connected to Soul from a root level.

Japan Law Twin Crystal – "V" shaped crystalline structure joined to form two definitive, often identical domains. This is a contact crystal as opposed to a penetrator crystal. Some Japan Law Twin Crystals have large notches at the join, while others are barely noticeable, but always form a 90 degree angle. Japan Law Twin Crystals, although rare in itself, is the most common of the Law Twin Crystals. Spiritually, Japan Law Twins are known as the "Stone of Perpetuation" and are used to clear the auric field around the body to perfect the subtle or finer bodies.

Brazil Law Twin Crystal – Penetration twin. Much harder to determine twinning characteristics of a Brazil Law Twin because the left and right twin aspect are within one single crystal. This type of twinning occurs in double terminated crystals and will have adjoined, sequential mirrored faces from top to bottom. Spiritually, Brazil Law Twin Crystals assist us in seeing within ourselves to connect with our highest purpose.

Dauphine Law Twin Crystal – Penetration Twin. Difficult to determine because the left and right twin aspects are within one single crystal. Occurs in double terminated quartz crystals and is evidenced by the mirror, sequential appearance of the side facets. Dauphine Law Twin Crystals help us to go with the flow of life, recognize patterns and make adjustments as suits our Highest Purpose.

Window Crystal – has a diamond-shaped 'window' located just below the tip of the crystal (between the main six faces forming its own smaller diamond shaped face). Powerful teaching tools, these crystals are used to transmit information through meditation and contemplation of the window. Clairvoyance, divination, psychic crystal. Windows offer highly charged literal views to Soul and to the Higher Self for a divinely intuitive connection that bypasses ego.

Yang Crystal – clear crystal, like glass. Masculine energies that build self-confidence, accomplish goals and eliminate victimization.

Yin Crystal – cloudy crystal, opaque – softness, feminine energies, receptive and gentle.

Yin/Yang Crystal – crystal that is balanced with both clarity and opacity. Brings about balance of male/female energies, teaching to give and receive.

METAPHYSICAL PROPERTIES OF CRYSTALS, ROCKS AND STONES

Here is a comprehensive list of the metaphysical properties of crystals and stones by Mineral compiled from many different sources online, offline, from personal experience and from information channeled through my guides who have helped me extensively. The use of crystals and stones in healing goes far back into our history to native peoples who through experimentation and discovery recognized the healing properties of different minerals.

Healing with crystals and stones is affected by intent. If we look to reduce something, such as anxiety, fever, pain or even weight loss, it is imperative that we be clear in our intent to negate. By being clear with negative intent, the crystals and/or stones will carry our intent as a deficit.

If our intent is to improve or increase something, such as improve our awareness or increase our confidence level, it is imperative that we focus our intent on positivity. Again, by being perfectly clear in our positive intent, the crystals and/or stones we use will heighten and empower our intent toward a positive result. Our intent is tantamount to achieving the desired result.

Please be absolutely clear as to what you wish to achieve.

Each rock, crystal, mineral or stone below has a corresponding ailment or issue that it addresses; many stones are multi-dimensional meaning they work on different issues on multiple levels. Each represents a traditional method of healing either through increase or decrease in energy associated with the stone in relation to the issue.

We encourage you to begin to accumulate different rocks and stones for your metaphysical toolbox, to 'make friends' with different rocks and stones. Quartz crystal is always a good choice, because it is universal in its empowerment and multidimensionality.

Crystals, Rocks and Stones are listed alphabetically, followed by a brief description of types of crystals and then crystal formations and their metaphysical meaning.

~

Agate – (multiple colors – variegated) enhances love, abundance, wealth, good luck, longevity, harmony; protector of children. Grounds to earth. One of the oldest stones in recorded history, it belongs to the variegated chalcedony group. Helps to change our level of perception; gives wearer the strength to carry on.

Agate, Blue Lace (blue with white streaks) -- Helpful in treating arthritis. Promote acceptance of miracles! Helps to heal wounds. Offers inspiration for inner healing and knowledge of inner self. Excellent choice to create an Angel stone.

Agate, Botswana (gray and pink) – Assists in fertility, sensuality and creative expression. Also protects anyone who works around smoke and/or fire, such as firemen, smokers, forestry workers. If you are looking to quit smoking, this is the stone to help you.

Agate, Crazy Lace – (orange. Yellow, white, blue) – Excellent tool to balance the senses, and absorb negativity, including emotional pain. Good stone for focus, excellent for those who suffer from attention disorders.

Agate, Eagle Eye – (brown, gold) - Helps one to rise above the day-to-day aspects of drudge and routine to see the larger picture of things. A wonderful stone for grounding one to earth, while giving a higher perspective – perfect stone of duality, affording two views. Enhances longevity.

Agate, Fire – (red, brown, orange) – Wonderful tool for removal of fear; hastens courage and strength to those who lack. Repels gossip and sends threats of harm back to the sender. Not a tool for play, this stone means business. Wear close to skin, near heart chakra to balance male and female energies.

Agate, Green Moss – (green with light blue) Success, abundance and prosperity stone. Good for friendships and maintaining balance amongst friends. Helps with self-esteem issues.

Agate, Moss (green, yellow, golden)- Known as the 'gardener's stone', moss agate lends an air of a green thumb to the wearer. It is believed that this stone helps to ensure a full and healthy crop for the farmer. It is also a stone of abundance and prosperity.

Agate, Orbital – (white, red, brown) – aka Eye or Cat's Eye Agate. Seer's stone, helps to focus and see beyond what is visible. Helps to discern right from wrong. Stone of protection and strength.

Agate, Tree - (green and white) – Beautiful stone, aka "Dendritic" agate. A wonderful tool for farmers and gardeners because it is believed to bring bountiful crops. Place in flower beds, and near house plants for beautiful blooms. Metaphysically assists one in widening their perspective and looking deeper into one's self for introspection and self-discovery.

Ajoite (blue-green) – extremely rare stone of high metaphysical property. Usually found with or connected to Papagoite and on quartz. Ajoite is often mistaken for Papagoite; however, Papagoite is blue, whereas Ajoite is green. Believed to remove psychically placed implants from the psyche, therefore returning and/or increasing one's ability to stand in their own power. Promotes peace and harmony though out the emotional body; heals old wounds and opens channels to encourage inner growth. Makes the connection between heart and throat energy centers in the body giving impetus to speaking what is in one's heart. Originally found in Ajo, Arizona, a second pocket was located in Messina, South Africa but has since closed due to instability of the physical environment of the mine. If you can get even a small piece of authentic Ajoite for your metaphysical toolbox, please do so as this mineral is on the extinction list.

2012 will simply enhance the metaphysical properties of this stone to remove negativity and psychically placed implants. Ajoite protects the wearer or user from implants being placed, as well as removes those already in place. And 2012 energies will also bring online a new, small source of true Ajoite which may drive the prices up even more.

Energies from Ajoite are extremely soft and gentle, pure energies from Source. 2012 and thereafter brings a furthering of these metaphysical enhancements that will continue to grow until on into the 22nd century. This stone helps to release anger, hurts and past life blockages and will continue to act as a bridge between dimensions, particularly more so in the New Age.

Albite – see Feldspar

Alexandrite (purple, red, green - color change) – a form of chrysoberyl, alexandrite appears green or bluish-green in daylight, and turns a soft shade of red, purplish-red or raspberry red in incandescent light. This is a stone of balance that helps one to flow with change. Also it acts as a stone of success bringing happiness to the wearer from work endeavors. Enhanced 2012 properties intensify feelings of accomplishment in career, love, relationships and sensuality. Increases self-esteem.

Alunite (clear to orange with dark purple figuring)) - helps to balance yin/yang energies and environmental energies. Takes unbalanced energies and transforms them to stabilizing and grounding energies. Also known as *Angel Wing*. Enhanced properties for 2012 and thereafter increase and improve one's abilities to rise above physical abnormalities and see the big picture, how things fit into the puzzle of life. Very good stone for those who may suffer from personality disorders in the physical.

Amazonite (Light blue-green) - bestows truth, sincerity, and honor. Improves eloquence in speaking from the heart. Associated with the throat chakra; relieves stress, and calms the nervous system. Aligns physical and soul bodies. Excellent balance for female energy. Enhanced empowerments for 2012 and thereafter increase and improve one's ability to speak their own truth in a productive way. Stabilizes feminine power. *Word of Caution: Contains traces of copper which is toxic. Do not add to drinking water. Use as etheric elixir.*

Amber – (Yellow to orange) - brings love, purification and wisdom; lifts depression, draws out negative energy and changes it into positive energy. Very soothing energies that both calm and energize at the same time, albeit gently. Works with endocrine system to purify the body, releasing toxins. Stabilizes kundalini energies. *Word of Caution: Contains potentially toxic dust or fumes. Do not add to drinking water. Use as etheric elixir.*

The New Age post-2012 brings with it enhanced metaphysical abilities of Amber, that have lain dormant waiting to be released. The golden doorway to the past is opening wider and wider as we approach 2012 and will remain open for Amber, allowing the wisdom of its captures to flourish. Light and Energy

Workers worldwide will be able to utilize these enhanced empowerments for the good of the whole as suits the All That Is.

Amethyst – (Dark to light purple) - increases spiritual awareness, meditative and psychic abilities, transforms negative energy into positive energy. Helps to release unwanted habits and release addictions. Promotes inner peace and assists in healing, relieving head problems. Instrumental in releasing old hurts. Activates Crown Chakra energy center. One of seven components of *Super Seven Crystal*.

Powerful changes are occurring in the metaphysical use of Amethyst for 2012 and thereafter.

Amethyst has long been used to balance the grieving process and heal physical/emotional hurts. Recent increase in frequency and vibration in crystals, rocks and stones has made a vast increase in the metaphysical properties of Amethyst.

Amethyst is being used to improve psychic abilities, deepen meditative state and promote more profound inner peace, serenity and tranquility. Held to the Brow Chakra (Spiritual Inner Eye or Tisra T'il), one increases their bio-magnetic energies to reach into higher frequencies of light and sound.

Amethyst brings clarity to the user, improved vision into the psychic realms and helps with questions about love and relationships.

In matters of the heart, Amethyst brings clarity of purpose and intent. Want to know if your lover is the right one for you? Hold an Amethyst in your hand and ask the question silently to yourself. You may feel a change in vibration physically -- relative to the answer to your question (slower for less likely and faster for more likely).

Amethyst has always been thought of as the stone of spirituality and contentment, bringing stability, strength and invigoration to the user. It is an energy of balance and common sense that the user will feel on an esoteric level ~~ very encouraging over the coming period of Earth Changes post-2012.

Ametrine (Purple and yellow) - stimulates the intellect, clears negativity from the aura and releases energy center blockages. Helps with soul and astral travel. Heals digestive disorders. Additional metaphysical use for 2012 and thereafter is to promote nutritional absorption with less food consumption – to help the body assimilate more nutritive value of consumed foods while lessening the amount of material waste created by the body. This will be an incredible discovery in the New Age.

Ammonite – (fossil) promotes domesticity, house keeping, cleaning and organization. Added to its use in 2012 and thereafter, Ammonite will help with bridging the gap between past lives, helping to bring forward valuable lessons that are helpful for today.

Andalusite (yellow, brown) – stone of clarity and balance. Good stone for metaphysicians because it assists in seeing clearly and without bias. Additional use in 2012 and thereafter, Andalusite can be used as a Harvest stone, helps one with reaping what they have sown both in the physical plane with gardens and crops, and also on the inner planes with studies, higher learning and spiritual growth.

Angelite (Light blue) -- Also known as Blue Anhydrite. Helps with contacting your Angels and Guides. Increases telepathy. Stone for peace, fellowship and brotherhood. Known as a team building stone. Hold this stone to your Tisra T'il (Third Eye Chakra) to improve your inner vision and connect with your Higher Self. *Word of Caution: May contain traces of lead and sulphur. Do not add to drinking water. Use as etheric elixir.*

Apache Tears (Obsidian) (black) - for physical and spiritual protection. Protects against depression and blocks negativity. Good stone for the gentle of heart because it offers strength and protection.

Apatite (Blue) - useful in intellectual pursuits, fosters communication, concentration and clarity of thought. Encourages extroversion, dissolves alienation, and draws away negativity. Good stone for arthritis sufferers because it is said to relieve joint pain. Its use in 2012 and thereafter is increasing the positive energy flow of other crystals and stones. This is an excellent stone to keep along side quartz crystal because it will enhance the vibratory rate of the quartz.

Apophyllite (clear, translucent) - Tetrahedral formations that look similar to clear quartz, but are actually a form of silica dioxide. Excellent to promote meditative state because its form and shape pull in positive energy. Also used to draw out negative energy. This is a stone that promotes happiness and joy in the user, which also makes it a perfect tool for those who suffer from depression.

Aqua Aura Crystals (clear with blue/green opalescence) (See Aura Crystals below) - Clear quartz crystals are electrically infused with gold to create this powerful crystal. Excellent psychics' stone, helpful with meditation, clairvoyancy, Reiki healing and energy work. Aids in increasing awareness. Works in concert with the throat chakra energy center. Good communicator's stone, excellent for public speakers, teachers, and anyone who addresses groups. Keep one in your pocket during oral exams, or speaking engagements to ward off inadvertent negativity from others.

Aquamarine (very pale blue) - associated with the calming effect of the sea, used to soothe, calm and alleviate fears. Used in communicating with aquatic life, even if one lives far from the sea Useful for deep meditations and contemplations. Can be used as an eye to inner worlds; when placed on Tisra T'il (third eye chakra), allows one to travel to the inner worlds in a protective bubble to experience, learn, and assist as necessary.

Aragonite (purple-pink) – hexagonal needle crystals ~ a healers' stone. Used for deep meditations and for balance yin-yang energies. This stone has grounding energies. Helpful for feminine energy, providing a window to your feminine side, especially for men or those with higher male energies.

Atlantisite (green with purple/blue) – Combination of Serpentine and Stichtite, discovered in Tasmania and named "Atlantisite" by Gerald Pauley, this unusual stone is a healer for the heart, lungs, stomach and kidneys. A good stone for women that is said to relieve complications of female disorders and relax cramping in the female organs. Found in Tasmania, Australia, Canada, Morocco, Scotland and South Africa, Atlantisite is believed to be a remnant from Atlantis that was used for healing female energy. This is a gentling stone, soothing to agitated spirits and hearts, Atlantisite also creates a sense of calm in whatever atmosphere it is housed. Important element to remove doubts and operates as a 'guardian crystal' to protect not only physically, but up through the multi-universes to protect you in the higher planes.

Aura Crystals – crystals created through a man-made process that involves infusing pure mineral vapors over quartz crystal. Pure gold vapors create Aqua Aura, platinum and silver vapors create Angel and Opal Aura, pure iron vapors create Solar Aura; pure Indium vapors create Rainbow Aura. Combination Aura crystals create more powerful stones --

Aura, Apple – nickel vapors fused to quartz crystal creates this powerful aura crystal. Good luck and fortune are attributed to this crystal.

Aura, Christ Commune Crystal™ (Aqua and Angel/Opal Aura) - a stone of deep joy and contentment that opens the heart of the user more deeply. Connects one to the Christ Consciousness.

Aura, Earth Synergizer crystals - a combination of Champagne Aura and clear Quartz Crystal that promotes balance with a multidimensional significance.

Aura, Flame / Rainbow crystals – enhanced crystal which has had titanium and niobium layered on top by electrostatic charge, producing a beautiful red rainbow effect that changes color in the light. Said to encourage soul mating and help one to find true love. Excellent stone of creative passion.

Aura, Self-Synergizer crystals - a combination of Aqua Aura and clear Quartz crystal and promotes DNA repair.

Aura, Solar Christ Commune crystals - a combination of Aqua Aura and Solar Aura and supports intense change.

Aura, Solar Goddess crystal - a combination of Solar Aura and Angel/Opal Aura; intensifies the Divine Feminine energy.

Aura, Angel - intensifies angel connection, and opens the communication pathway between user and the angels. Always remember to be specific when contacting the angels.

Aura, Solar - creates a Solar Vortex that can be used to heal the deepest wounds of the human psyche, as well as increasing joy and the feeling of wholeness and wellness.

Aura, Rainbow - promotes high multidimensional energies.

Aura Merkaba, Violet Flame of Count St. Germain – A merkaba star is hand cut by crystal artisans and looks like one pyramid inverted over another pyramid, forming an eight-pointed three dimensional star. The Violet Flame Merkaba is most powerful in opening one up to the Violet Flame energies that Count St. Germain brought forward concerning spiritual healing and enlightenment. The Violet Flame of Count St. Germain Merkaba is working with 2012 energies to enhance the process of ascension by fully activating the Light Body. The process of Ascension has already begun and this beautiful crystal merkaba has undergone an alchemical process of infusing gold and indium on the crystal to totally restructure the metaphysical properties of the stone.

The merkaba spins in a counter-rotating field of light that enhances the ascension experience of body, mind and spirit. It represents the vehicle in which spirit moves through the dimensions.

Aventurine (green, orange, blue, yellow, gray) - creativity, imagination, prosperity, career success and balance. Related to heart chakra energy center. Believed to be 'good luck' stone for gamblers and lotto players. Keep stone in left pocket and you will always have money, it's been said. In its green form, it is also known as *Fuschite*.

Green Aventurine is the stone of the Heart Energy Center, opening the doorway to love and compassion. This stone is beautiful whether it is polished or in its rough with its tiny flecks of quartz that give it such a beautiful sparkle.

Its metaphysical purpose acts as the integrator between opposites, connecting mind and body, male and female, ego and spirit. It is a stone of harmony within the Self, which sparks a connection with creativeness by the user.

Azeztulite™ (clear to snowy white) – Said to be a stone first discovered in North Carolina and then later in Vermont; however, claims have been that the mines have closed making the stone unavailable and extremely pricey. Research has shown that many believe the stone was a gift from the Azez alien race.

Metaphysical properties of Azeztulite™ are deepening of clairvoyancy, projecting positive energy, rejuvenates cells at a biomolecular level, expands and raises consciousness.

Word of caution: What is being offered as Azeztulite™ quite often is simply common white quartz because they look exactly alike, the difference being the vibration and sound frequency of the stone. Azeztulite™ is said to have a very high vibratory and frequency rate, and one must be prepared to work with it. It is also believed that Azeztulite™ is a stone for the New Age, bringing with it spectacular healing abilities to the user and a direct uplink through to the dimensions and interdimensional beings.

However, Azeztulite™ has been the subject of internet scams; use caution and purchase from reputable dealers only. Azeztulite™ is the trademark of Heaven and Earth LLC, and asserts Trade and Copyright protection for the name Azeztulite™

Azurite (indigo, electric blue) - promotes clear understanding, cleansing, healing, purification, purpose, kindness, patience, prophecy and truth. Aids in psychic travel. Useful during meditation. Held in front of brow / third eye chakra energy center, this stone will help to open inner vision. Stimulates the liver and aids detoxification of organs. Good for thyroid gland. *Word of Caution: Contains traces of copper which is toxic. Do not add to drinking water. Use as etheric elixir.*

Beryl (green) – also known as Emerald. Enhances intellectual abilities, wisdom. Prophecy stone. Used to make elixirs to heal eye problems and eyesight troubles. High vibratory rate that enhances love.

Bixbite (Red beryl) - Also known as red or scarlet emerald. This is an extremely rare stone known to be found in very few locations in the Western United States. Stone has been used to strengthen creativity and bring harmony to relationships. Has been used to heal physical problems related to cardiovascular system.

Black Obsidian - change, transformation, metamorphosis, fulfillment, inner growth. Grounding energy to physical plane.

Black Tourmaline (black) -- Repels and protects against negativity. If you have been exposed to radiation, this stone will absorb it. Also instrumental in returning negative energy, black magic and voodoo back to where it came from.

Bloodstone – (green with red spots) A green jasper tinged with iron oxide that enhances alignment, organization and energy flow. Healing stone for dis-ease, ailments and illness that impact the physical body. Removes emotional and physical blockages. This is also a stone for survivors and helps with endurance beyond the norm.

Blue Quartz (blue) – Also known as "Dumortierite', is a tool of self-discipline known to enhance organizational abilities of the wearer. Works with the throat chakra energy center for balance in communication. Brings a sense of order and balance to the wearer; enhance clarity of thought and lifts depression. Good tool for students and those who are taking on a new course of study.

2012 enhancements increase balance and order, and assist with downloading information through the dimensions.

Blue Topaz (blue) -- Stimulating to throat chakra energy center; good for speakers, helps to clear communication obstacles and see things as balanced. Brings us closer to Universe and Collective.

Bornite - (Brownish-violet) aka Peacock Ore. This stone is copper-colored to a brownish color when first unearthed. After exposure to the elements, it tarnishes to blue, red and purple. At this stage, Bornite is called "Peacock Ore." Oftentimes, what is being sold as 'Peacock Ore' is heavily tarnished Chalcopyrite that has been artificially enhanced with acid. Exposing Chalcopyrite to acid produces a high flash tarnish that shimmers and perhaps may be mistaken as Peacock Ore.

Bornite is known as a 'happiness stone' that holds a very high frequency of energy. Use Bornite to receive a high power infusion of spiritual energy, to open the Tisra T'il. Also affects some users physically, being perceived as a mild rush of energy. This stone is excellent at aligning the body's energy centers and helps one to move forward into the high realms. Helps to remove that which we no longer need.

The metaphysical purpose of Bornite is increasing in 2012 and beyond. A stone for the 'now', Bornite is being charged with perpetual movement of spirit between the dimensions, so that the user actually pulses nanosecond to nanosecond between the two. Is most beneficial in dream state so that the physical self can move between worlds with complete protection. Will be used for time travel as well as dimensional travel. *Word of Caution: Contains traces of copper and sulphur that are toxic. Do not add to drinking water. Use as etheric elixir. See Chalcopyrite.*

Boji™ Stones – aka *Kansas Pop Rock. Boji™ Stones* were 'discovered' by Karen Gillespie on her property in Gove County, Kansas. Boji™ Stones are unusual in that they are come in pairs, one male and one female. There are also androgynous Boji™ Stones which carry both energies. Boji™ Stones are receiving activations on a daily basis, gearing up to take their rightful place as the Stone for the New Age, or as they have been referred to as "The Stone of Humanity."

Boji™ Stones and/or Kansas Pop Rocks are said to facilitate moving energies between the physical and higher dimensional bodies, helping to keep the bodies in balance. Also, they are intensive activators for alignment of the chakra energy system. Physically, Boji™ Stones are electrical conductors that impact the body's auric field, enhancing conductivity. Also, Boji™ Stones are believed to draw off pain, helping the body to process it harmlessly.

An interesting observation of a Kansas Pop Rock is its odor. There is an aura of sulfur that emanates from the stone – not unpleasant – just unmistakable, which is reminiscent of the open pools in Yellowstone National Park. These stones are a wonderfully energetic concretion of iron sulfide, marcasite and pyrite, hence the slight odor. *Word of Caution: May contain toxic sulphur. Do not add to drinking water. Use as etheric elixir.*

These stones are called "Pop Rocks" because they 'pop' when thrown into a fire, and give off sparks when hit together.

These are beautiful additions to your metaphysical toolbox, whether you acquire a certified Boji™ Stone or Kansas Pop Rocks, I know you will enjoy the energies.

Bronze - relaxation, serenity, calmness; promotes a laid-back attitude. Good for grounding and keeping one in the physical reality. Metaphysical purpose increases in 2012 and beyond, reaching back into its historical use as a protector, Bronze rises to its use to repulse negativity like a protective shield. Will be used to create etheric protective shields for when one travels through the dimensions.

Bustamite (Pink, Red, Brown with Sugalite) - Removes energy blockages and realigns the energy centers. Helps to clear heart energy center and promotes a calming atmosphere in the middle of chaos. Useful in meditation and contemplation because it promotes the creation of a sacred space where Soul and the Inner Be-ingness is held in highest esteem. Good dreamers' stone.

Cacoxenite – (brownish gold and purple) is useful in assisting spiritual evolution. Said to expand consciousness, helps to align the solar plexus chakra or energy center, assists in emotional upheaval and cleanses one of negative attachments. Also used to heal stomach disorders and offers thyroid support. One of seven components of Super Seven Crystal a/k/a Melody's Stone.

Calcite – (Clear) attuned to the mental plane. Used to strengthen against mental anguish and inner turmoil. Associated with the metaphysical, enhances spirituality; enhances healing abilities. Amplification of energies. Micro-crystals of calcite are contained within the inner ear and the pineal gland, which resonate in accordance with our light, sound and color frequencies. 2012 activations enhance the physical electrical charge of calcite increasing our abilities to hear, see, feel and sense resonances in frequency and vibration within and without our bodies. Calcite will help to bring us forward through the dimensions via higher plane travel and soul journeys.

Calcite – Blue – soothing energies that calm and bring a sense of peace to one's atmosphere. As with all Calcite, Blue Calcite amplifies energies and is very good for those who have trouble communicating their thoughts to others. Works with throat chakra energy center. Amplifies energy, helps in dream recollection and soul travel experiences from dream state. Channelers' stone; clears and activates throat chakra energy center.

Calcite – Green – stone for prosperity and financial success. Amplifies intuition and psychic abilities; works with heart chakra energy center to improve and stabilize relationships.

Calcite – Honey -- sweet energy that gently enhances and amplifies energy of other stones; acts as an assistant. Honey Calcite enables us to accept and use change to our best advantage.

Calcite – Orange -- Works with sacral energies to strengthen core properties of the body. 2012 energies offer enhancements to multidimensional connection and amplification of communion through the dimensions.

Calcite – Pink -- soft, gentle healing energies, useful with Reiki. Very calming to the spirit, opens and facilitates the heart chakra energy center. Mothering, nurturing stone that soothes and comforts.

Calcite – Red -- detoxifying, healing energy, that increases inner strength and amplifies stability. Helps to ease and release fears. Works with root chakra energy center. Excellent tool for balancing love life difficulties.

Calcite – Yellow – solar plexus stimulant works with clearing away blockages in the solar plexus energy center. Stimulates physical energies; good stone to accompany you during strenuous activities. If you have trouble meditating, this stone brings meditative state into focus and perspective Known to amplify energy, this is a channelers' stone, amplifies soul travel experiences. Stone works with DNA and spinal column to support connection between physical and spiritual planes.

Calcite – Fluorescent – color change stone that helps one to recognize and work with winds of change. Fluorescent Calcite is a clear or opalescent stone that glows when exposed to artificial light sources.

Calcite – Citrine – gently works to soothe digestive tract; acts as an enhancer to nourishing foods. 2012 and beyond activation for Citrine Calcite: Place Citrine Calcite next to your food to amplify the body's ability to receive nutrients.

Calcite – Aqua -- Similar energies to Blue Calcite, but more subtle. Acts as an emotional protector.

Calcite – Tangerine – Often striped with clear Calcite. Mellow and comforting energy. Good as a psychic enhancer and amplifier.

Calcite – Rainbow – Represents our multidimensionality. 2012 enhancements to create unification between physical (3D) and higher dimensions (4D and above).

Carnelian - enhances energy flow, creativity, courage, happiness, self-esteem and memory. Stone for harvesting dreams and things we dream. Excellent stone for those in the field of acting and performing. Known as a Thespian's Stone.

Catlinite: *See Pipestone.*

Cat's Eye - (aka "Tiger's Eye" – golden brown) builds determination, strength of mind, will power, moral turpitude. Cat's Eye is often referred to as "chatoyant" or that it has 'chatoyancy' meaning that it resembles the eye of a cat. This 'chatoyancy' amplifies the users ability to see more deeply into things, and give the user strength in manipulating their atmosphere to obtain what is needed and desired.

Cavansite – (bright royal blue) great stone to increase and improve psychic abilities; stimulating to intuitive thought processes, heightens psychic awareness and stimulates brow chakra (spiritual third eye.) Excellent healers tool because it not only promotes healing, it also protects the healer as well.

Celestite (shades of blue) – Beautiful stone of peace heightens spiritual development, enlightenment, awareness. Encourages and facilitates petition or prayer; aids channeling with other beings, angels, spirit guides. Wonderful choice for creating an angel stone. Used to expand creative energy, in 2012 and beyond, Celestite will form a better fit between humans and their angel guides, in attracting guides to a person and in contact.

Chalcedony – (blue, pink) vitality, stamina and endurance; energizing effect on people and things. Stone of peace with subtle vibration, giving healing on multiple levels to user. Used by indigenous peoples during ceremonies to connect with higher realms. 2012 activations bring enhancement to mind, body, and spirit connectivity.

Chalcopyrite -(yellow) This stone is sometimes referred to as "Peacock Ore" after it has been heavily tarnished.

Peacock Ore is the term given to tarnished Bornite, but usually, what you are seeing or getting is Chalcopyrite with a heavy tarnish, turning the copper from yellow to bluish-purple.

Metaphysical use of Chalcopyrite include the ability to clear the spiritual third eye chakra and throat chakra, improve psychic ability and the ability to reach beyond. Chalcopyrite is a psychic's stone.

Chalcopyrite is a most beautiful stone with its intense sparkle of blue, purple and pink.

It is used quite often as a meditation tool and in directing the flow of the Universal Life Force with Reiki. Metaphysically, Peacock Ore helps to dislodge spiritual blockages and is often used for clarity of spirit when held near the Third Eye (Brow Chakra).

Also, this is a 'Psychic's Stone" because it is believed to help those who are clairvoyant or remote viewers to "see" with their Spiritual Eye more clearly by enhancing inner knowing and strengthening perception. Those who are psychically inclined usually love this mineral, not only for its beauty, but for its ability to enhance and promote trust in what they see, hear and feel psychically.

When I am looking for clarity, I like to hold a piece of Chalcopyrite to my brow and 'listen'.

Also, alternative practitioners use this mineral as a healing stone and protector against asthma, lung disorders and throat (communication) difficulties. *See Bornite. Word of Caution: Contains traces of copper and sulphur which are toxic. Do not add to drinking water. Use as etheric elixir.*

Charoite – (purple/blue/lilac) Known as a stone of transformation and power, Charoite is useful to transform anger and fear into positive feelings; releases negativity and inspires enhanced creativity and spiritual growth. A 'victim's' stone, it enhances courage and inner strength.

Chiastotlite (brown with black cross) – known as 'cross stone', this is a stone of protection that turns disharmony into harmony. Good for change and balances perception.

Chlorite (clear, white, green, gray) – Powerfully strong healing stone that cleanses and purifies the aura, and the body's energy centers. Excellent stone to remove unwanted energy implants that works to correct the negative void that is left after the implant is removed. Also used to remove physical toxins from the body. This is an unsung hero in the war against negativity, particularly hostility and anger.

Chrysoberyl (Yellow, green, reddish-brown) - builds kindness, generosity, forgiveness and benevolence. This is a stone of protection and has been used by ancient civilizations as a protector to keep away disaster and negativity. Helps to open crown chakra and aligns the chakras from the crown to the solar plexus. See Alexandrite and Cymphane.

Chrysocolla - (greenish-blue) tranquility, serenity and peace; represents the water element; revitalizes lower charkas. Purification of home. Looks similar to turquoise and has many of the same physical qualities yet, the energies are quite different. Chrysocolla has been charged with being a stone of wisdom, but in 2012 it undergoes metamorphosis to become a teacher of ancient knowledge. It will be used to download ancient wisdom to those seekers who possess the 'key' to unlocking its records. The 'key' comes in dream state when the student is ready. *Word of Caution: Contains traces of copper which is toxic. Do not add to drinking water. Use as etheric elixir.*

Chrysoprase – (minty green) balance, promoting stability, expression and communication. Patron of children, young animals and seedlings. Chrysoprase is a healing stone that works with the eyes, and metaphysically helps to open the Tisra T'il, third eye chakra. 2012 brings an anticipated upgrade to its healing powers for eyesight, migraine headaches caused by thickening of the blood, and drawing off pain caused by neuralgia and nerve degeneration.

Cinnabar – (deep red) Also known as *"Dragonstone,"* Origin of liquid mercury. Metaphysical representation of vitality, energetic ability, and assertiveness.

Enhanced properties for New Age (2012 and thereafter) for channeling aggressive tendencies into a more productive assertiveness. Good stone for introverts willing to adjust persona or change image. Helps user to wield power in a productive, positive manner; takes the edge off those with forceful personalities, making them more aesthetically pleasing with an air of elegance. *Word of Caution: Contains mercury which is toxic and transferable to skin. Do not add to drinking water. Use as etheric elixir.*

Citrine – (yellow) -- stimulates earthly pleasure, protection, strength and confidence; healing to digestive tract and eases emotional imbalance. Associated with Solar Plexus Chakra. Newly activated as a diet and metabolism stone.

Beautiful citrine is a passionate yellow stone that has been used to clear the spiritual aura because it purifies and dissipates negativity, bringing about a state of positivity.

Citrine is connected to the stomach and digestive system (Solar Plexus Chakra) and enhances the body's metabolism. Those who are interested in balancing their metabolism, or desirous of losing weight do very well when working with a Citrine.

One of the enhanced energies of Citrine is to balance the digestive system. Holding a Citrine in your hand while you bless your food and/or water will energize it with Universal Life Force energies allowing your body to fully utilize active minerals, trace elements and available nutrition.

Placing a Citrine in your drinking water for a period of 12 to 24 hours will turn a simple glass of water into a miraculous gem infused elixir that will send healing throughout your digestive tract and system. CAUTION: Before drinking, remove any crystals or stones.

Citrine also will help with flushing toxins from the stomach, liver, gallbladder and spleen. It balances the thyroid and activates the thymus gland, purifying the essence of the Self.

USING CITRINE AS A DIET STONE:

Keep citrine with you at all times if you are choosing to use it as a 'diet stone'. It will give you strength to resist the urge to eat things that are not good for you. Make an elixir with your diet citrine to help your metabolism by placing a stone in your water container' this will also aid in the assimilation of nutrients.

Use polished citrine, not rough, and make sure it is at least 2 inches in size so it cannot be swallowed. Drink this elixir every day and sip on it all day long.

To power up your household water, place a citrine on top of your water heater or conditioner. Place a 2 inch polished citrine in the water pitcher before you fill it with water.

Citrine is a wonderful cleanser and purifier for the endocrine and digestive system. It helps to eliminate toxins and poison from the system. It also is a powerful soother and calmer to a taxed digestive system, particularly when one is under stress. Citrine is an excellent tool to ease depression as well as digestive problems. It is a good stone for diabetics and for those who suffer from elimination troubles, constipation, and/or frequent diarrhea.

I am suggesting a polished citrine because it will not break down like a rough stone might when jostled around in water.

Word of Caution: Do not use small stones. Stone must be at least 2 inches if being added to drinking water so there will not be a choking hazard. In order to fully remove any chance of a choking hazard, place the stone next to the bottle or glass of water before you drink it and instruct the stone to act in the manner it would if it were placed in the water.

Cobalt (blue) - fosters channeling, communication with higher beings, meditation, balance, prayer and thankfulness. *Word of Caution: Cobalt is toxic. Do not add to drinking water. Use as etheric elixir.*

Combarbalita -- (rusty brown with beige, yellow and white) This semi-precious stone mined in the area around Combarbala, Chile, and is the native stone of Chile. Combarbalita is a beautiful stone, similar in structure and appearance to marble, which is often tooled by Chilean artisans into sculptures and figurines.

Combarbalita was formed over 80 thousand years ago by volcanic eruptions and depending upon the type of minerals in the area of its creation determines the beautiful coloration. You will most often see Combarbalita with swirls of cream, white and brown marbling in a reddish base. This coloration is caused by a mixture of red hematite and kaolin. Turquoise Combarbalita was formed from a mixture of kaolin (white chalky stone) and schlossmacherite (green triagonal stone) at the time of its formation.

Knowledge of the metaphysical properties of Combarbalita is relatively new and being downloaded to practitioners now in the Age of Aquarius so that this stone can begin its journey as a medicinal/spiritual tool. I received this information in meditation to pass along to those interested in working with this stone.

Combarbalita is related to the Root Chakra. Those that are emotionally weak, or unable to make decisions would do well to carry this stone with them. It is a good stone to use as a paperweight on your desk where decision-making is important. This is a very powerful stone for fire signs – Aries, Leo, Sagittarius. Since it was born of a powerful explosion of earth elements, Combarbalita assists the handler/user to make swift, deft decisions toward long sought after goals. When one is feeling weak due to illness or psychic attack, Combarbalita lends its gentle strength and substance of support and wards off negativity so that the body can heal.

A stable protector stone, Combarbalita draws off negative energy that is sent by others, whether intentional or unintentional.

Because of its hematite content, Combarbalita magnetizes and strengthens the user to stand up for themselves, improves confidence, and increases logical thinking threads.

Green Schlossmacherite lends the properties of healing, especially to the cardiac and circulatory system; Turquoise Combarbalita is associated with the Heart Chakra Center.

Copper - promotes channeling, cleansing, luck, prosperity, purification, self-esteem, facilitates the flow of energy. Used as a healing mineral due to its ability to conduct energy. *Word of Caution: Copper is toxic. Do not add to drinking water. Use as etheric elixir.*

Copper is used to draw pain away from joints and alleviate symptoms of cramps – hence you will often find copper being used in jewelry – bracelets and amulets.

Copper is also believed to energize the body both physically and emotionally by promoting the flow of oxygen when worn.

Coral – (pink, orange, red) balance, relaxation, protection, safety in travel on water. Ancient Egyptians used Coral to protect the souls of the departed in the afterlife. 2012 and thereafter, Coral comes online as an important component for emotional healing and uplifting emotions, helping one to rise above the walls of a self-made rut and get back into the groove of life. Coral brings enhanced peace and serenity with it into the New Age.

Covelite – (deep blue) Vision stone that increases psychic ability of the user. Helps in the expansion of knowledge and wisdom.

Cuprite – (metallic red) Helps with absorption of nutrients, and creates a calming, peaceful atmosphere for those who suffer from muscle cramping, and calcification. *Word of Caution: Contains traces of copper which is toxic. Do not add to drinking water. Use as etheric elixir.*

Cymophane (Light green to golden yellow) - also known as "Cat's Eye," a form of Chrysoberyl, has a delicate white opalescent stripe called 'chatoyancy' which lends to the 'cat's eye' effect. Dispels unwanted energy from aura, brings joy, serenity and happiness to wearer; transforms negative thought patterns to positive thought patterns through contemplation. Protects against evil.

Danburite - clear stone with crystal structure, amplification of other stones' effectiveness; releases energy blockages, causes healing on all levels.

Datolite (greenish-white) -- wonderful tool that can increase ones' stature. It helps with problem solving and brings a mental clarity that improves detail recall. Good for those in flux because it helps us to accommodate change in our lives.

Desautekite - clairvoyance, psychic abilities, fortune telling and seeing the future. Helps during divination. Wonderful psychic's tool because it helps to open the spiritual eye chakra with clarity.

Diamond (brilliant and clear) - bonds relationships, promotes hope and protects innocence; encourages love, abundance and courage. In the hands of a healer, diamond becomes a very powerful tool that intensifies healing energy. Excellent for Reiki and Energy workers. Once a diamond is possessed, it should never be lent to another because its healing and protective power will diminish.

Diopside (green) – Useful as a calmative, especially to animals, pets, small children and the elderly. Stimulates intellect, allows for focus and improves one's ability to understand their present circumstances with more clarity. *Word* *of Caution: May contain traces of copper which is toxic. Do not add to drinking water. Use as etheric elixir.*

Dioptase (deep blue green) – for the heart chakra energy center, helps to release sadness, and heal hurts of heartache, abuse and neglect. Encourages forward movement and ability to love deeply. Emotional balance. *Word of Caution: Contains traces of copper which is toxic. Do not add to drinking water. Use as etheric elixir.*

Dolomite (whitish-tan) – Stimulus for energetic thinking; excellent for brainstorming sessions. Provides endurance and stamina. Helps to realign energy centers and to return the system into balance.

Dumortierite (blue) – see Blue Quartz

Emerald – (green beryl) promotes clairvoyance and seeing by opening the spiritual third eye. Stone of Love. Empowers and balances while removing confusion. Pulls the wearer into the NOW and opens up the flow of deeper spiritual connection and insight. *Word of Caution: Emerald may contain aluminum which is toxic. Do not add to drinking water. Use as etheric elixir.*

Epidote - Pink and green - also known as Epidotized Granite or Unakite. This stone increases anything it touches whether energy or material matter. Lessens closed mindedness and causes one to focus more intently on that to which the wearer attunes. *See Unakite.*

Erythrite (crimson) -- Stimulates vital organs and infuses energy to one's self. Promote self-empowerment. Good talisman for speakers or those in a place of communication because it protects the throat and causes an unhindered flow of thought into word. Helpful with blood disorders.

Eudialyte (pink, red) – also known as *"Almandine"*, Eudialyte is a personal power stone that works with the wearer psychically by enhancing clairaudience, manifestation and psychic resonance. This is a good protective stone for anyone who works in the psychic arena. Brings harmony in love and relationships, dispels jealousy and brings the root and heart chakra into alignment. Eases compulsive behavior, so a good stone for anyone who suffers from obsessive/compulsive disorder.

Falcon's Eye (blue) – Also known as *Blue Tiger's Eye* and sometimes referred to as *Hawk's Eye*, this deep blue stone is used as a throat chakra energy center activator. Good stone for protection. Use in 2012 will enhance spoken communication skills of the user and promote visions.

Feldspar - (white, brown, gray) – said to offer tact to those who have little; supports courage and helps to eliminate fear. Used in history to treat eye disorders and metaphysically to give inner vision. 2012 activates enhancement to metaphysical properties.

Feldspar has many varieties and accessory minerals, to name a few: Oregon Sunstone, Garnet, Amazonite, Bornite, Chalcopyrite, Pyrite, Epidote, Malachite, Beryl, Mica, Quartz, Tourmaline, Thulite, Moonstone, among others.

Flint - (brown, black) - This stone is a variety of quartz, though usually darker in color than quartz. It is found in quantities all across the globe. Metaphysical properties including the prevention of night terrors and nightmares. Flint works with intellectual and psychological stimuli to provide insight into the 'unknown'. Stimulates tissue regeneration and heals injuries. Good for post-surgical recuperation.

Fluorite - Found in natural Octahedral formations, Fluorite is the psychic shield of protection, unblocks energy, also energizes and protects; truth, consciousness.

Blue Fluorite – Safety shield for eyes, ears, nose and throat;

Purple Fluorite -- aura cleanser and psychic protection;

Green Fluorite -- harmony and recharging chakra energy centers; improvement of financial picture.

Yellow Fluorite – fellowship and networkers stone;

Lavender Fluorite – peace of mind, serenity, connection to the Universes;

Rainbow Fluorite – stone of change; promotes well being, and helps one to get back on track, find their groove. Fluorite is an excellent stone for those with an entrepreneurial spirit.

Fuschite (green) – known as the Doctor Stone, Fuschite is used to heal the body by enhancing the body's ability to heal itself. Excellent stone for Reiki

Practitioners, Massage Therapists, Nurse Practitioners, Doctors and Surgeons. Often found to contain ruby.

Fulgurite – aka Prayer Pipe, Lechatelierite, Petrified Lightning; colors: black, tan, gray, white, brown – tubular in shape, this stone is a natural glass created by lightning strikes in sand and sometimes on rock. This is a high-energy stone, excellent for creating an Angel Stone. Metaphysical properties reach far back into ancient, Native wisdom. 2012 activations enhance communication properties through dimensions between user and sentient beings within the planes and Universes.

Galaxite – gray with colorful flash – Also known as 'micro-labrodite', Galaxite or Galaxyite is used as an aura stone. When you look at Galaxite, you'll notice multiple colorations, or 'flash' on the face of the stone. This 'flash' acts as a healer and cleanser to the auric field. In 2012 and beyond, Galaxite will become more and more useful as a transformational tool, helping in spiritual growth, mystical proliferation of intellectual pursuits, and projection of the Soul body through interdimensional travel.

Galena - shiny, silvery color - promotes healing, calmness sensitivity, insight. Used in Shamanic Healing. Not for use in Elixirs and not suggested as a tool for children because Galena is the primary source for lead. New use in 2012 is resonating harmonious vibrations in groups and bringing like-minded individuals closer together. *Word of Caution: Contains lead which is toxic. Do not add to drinking water. Use as etheric elixir.*

Garnet – (red) romantic love and passion, promotes sexuality; attracts love; past life recall. Improves self-confidence and increases courage. Also a good stone to stimulate business and success.

This beautiful stone is a deep burgundy color and hails as the birthstone for the month of January. Its metaphysical properties include confidence building and support, improvement of courage and bravery, Garnet is believed to encourage past life recall while helping to maintain balance in the now. It has also been called the 'jewel of love' because it is said to attract lovers and help love to flourish.

Those who suffer from depression would do well to carry a garnet in their metaphysical toolbox (or bag) because Garnet is believed to help relieve depression, improve self-esteem and remove negativity and fears from dream state.

Garnet also helps improve sexual drive and strengthens the sexual organs against disease. It is also thought to help women with hormone imbalance and hemorrhage, so is a good stone for 'monthly' woes, as well. This is a very powerful stone to use for healing emotional wounds. *Word of Caution: May contain traces of aluminum which is toxic. Do not add to drinking water. Use as etheric elixir.*

Gaspeite – (apple green w/brown or orange flecks) - Rare stone found in only two locations on Earth – the Gaspe Peninsula in Quebec, Canada and in Western Australia. Used by the Aborigines as a spiritual healing tool, this stone is found in and around nickel sulfide deposits. Said to be helpful with heart and lung problems; also healing to gall bladder issues. New use in 2012 and thereafter is to usher in spirituality as the norm in our daily lives, helping us to rise above the mundane and see the larger picture. In healing, Gaspeite protects the lungs and pulmonary system.

Geodes – volcanic stone - fosters intellectual insight, awareness, and community; helps to attract compatible friendships and lovers.

Girasol – light blue opalescent quartz – powerful energies surround the wearer, but in a very subtle, gentle way. 2012 and thereafter heralds new use for Girasol to enhance healing on multiple levels, from the physical on up through the dimensions.

Goethite (black, dark red, rust) – forms in stalactites - needle-like crystals and is often found near and around quartz. Stimulates psychic and metaphysical pursuits and aids in concentration. Said to raise consciousness and vibratory rate to enable clairaudient communication. Links one to the Angelic realm. Attuned to the sound of the Universe. One of seven components of the Super Seven Stone.

Gold - happiness, honor, strength of will, moral excellence, inspires virtue; balance, stability and grounding energy.

Granite - encourages to find your higher path and to live in the state of grace. Stone for emotional strength. Granite comes into its own power in 2012 and Beyond; stone for the New Age, empowering strength, endurance and vitality.

Green Millennium™--- New mineral find for the 21st Century, coming at a time of great need where the Earth is in crisis. Helps to bring balance and harmony back to lives that have been severely shaken by the Earth changes. Promotes higher purpose and emotionally detached focus. Works with Heart Chakra, changing non-cohesive energy into life affirming harmonious energy that starts the process of transformation and ascension.

Green Tourmaline (dark green) – success, wealth and abundance stone. Money magnet helps with bills and finances. Good for eyesight problems. Adds to effectiveness of herbal treatments.

Hematite (metallic dark gray) ~ promotes balance, focus, convergence and concentration of energy. Hematite has a very high vibratory rate that can be felt in the hand. Known to increase resistance to stress and enhances personal magnetism. *Word of Caution: Contains traces of iron which can rust. Do not add to drinking water. Use as etheric elixir.*

Herderite (Blue) – beautiful translucent blue crystal from Brazil. Used to connect to higher realms, supports and promotes interdimensional travel and expansion of consciousness. Welcomed by Spirit Guides and Light Beings, Herderite stimulates communication of a higher degree forming a mind link. Perfect stone for psychics, mediums, channelers and those seeking contact. This is a universal gateway stone.

Herkimer Diamond (clear) -- Great stone to boost and improve the energies of other stones. Looks similar in appearance to clear quartz crystal. Helps to release stress and tension in the body. Also wonderful amplifiers that turn up the power of energy in people, stones and in the atmosphere that we create.

Herkimer Diamonds are often found with anthracite inclusions, making them appear to look very much like Tibetan Tourmalinated Quartz. The difference quite often is that Herkimer Diamonds are more water clear and vibrate at a different frequency than Tibetan Quartz.

Herkimer Diamonds, like Tibetan Quartz, are double terminated, which means that they grow singularly and not on matrix. They began their lives within a vug or hole inside dolostone in a solution comprised of silicon dioxide about four million years ago.

Hiddenite (green) -- A variety of Spodumene, mined in North Carolina. Hiddenite is quite often gem quality and therefore costly; however, it is truly a beautiful stone, especially for energy workers since it operates openly from the

Heart Chakra Energy Center. *Word of Caution: May contain traces of aluminum which is toxic. Do not add to drinking water. Use as etheric elixir.*

Holey Stone (white, gray) – Also known as Holy Stone, Witches' Stone, Stone of Odin, Hag Stone and/or Fairy Stone, these beautiful pieces have been found around the shores of the Mediterranean, the northern Atlantic and many other waterside areas where the seas are rough enough to cause holes to form clear through rock. In ancient times, man-made holey stones were used in ceremonies for protection. Many different cultures recognize Holey Stones for their spiritual upliftment, spiritual protection and to carry them through the veil of physicality. Some Holey Stones are huge enough for people to walk through, and in some cultures it is believed that dis-eases and pain would be removed if one walked through a Holey Stone. The most sought after Holey Stones are nature-made, not man-made. Believed to prevent nightmares and protect the sleeping, they are also used for meditation and healing. Rub a natural Holey Stone over a place on the body where there is pain or illness, and it is said that one will be healed.

Howlite (gray) – extracts pain from the body. Increase balance and maintains focus; promotes networking. Has a calming effect on the user, reduces anger and stress. Used by indigenous peoples as a stone of protection.

Iolite (purple) -- Used in conjunction with the brow and crown chakra for healing and during guided meditations and soul / astral travel. Heightens spiritual growth; improves aura and stimulates shamanic visions. Powerful channeler and psychic stone. *Word of Caution: May contain traces of aluminum which is toxic. Do not add to drinking water. Use as etheric elixir.*

Jade (green) - serenity, wisdom, tranquility; unification of spiritual world and physical world. Stone of longevity, Jade's vibratory rate gently pulses a continual stream of energy outward from the wearer or user that may be directed inwardly, as well. Jade stands for humility and works very well as a Reiki stone because of its humble, gentle balance. Jade has been found in a variety of colors besides green – blue, black, violet, white, rust, yellow, cream, red, orange, and indigo are some of the variations.

Jasper - healing to Base (Root) Chakra, relaxation, contentment, mothering, nurturing, caring, comforting presence, Red – blood stone, root chakra energizer; Leopard Skin – connects you to your animal spirit guides; Rainbow – relaxes, reduces stress; Yellow – channels positive energy.

Jasper, Leopardskin – Wonderful stone to assist those who work in the public service arena; a community stone that brings like minded individuals together, attracts the like minded. Also helps with body odors, decreases body odors and eliminates toxins through the skin and from the body. 2012 energies place leopardskin jasper within the animal spirit realms where it operates from the highest level to assist in connecting to animal spirit guides.

Jasper, Rainbow Fantasy™ - (mix of colors from white to green to red to brown, purple, yellow, pink and blue) – This form of jasper was discovered in 2000 in the Sierra Madres Mountains in Mexico between Jalisco and Durango. Interesting designs from bull's eyes, orbic shapes and stripes occur naturally with no two pieced being alike. Metaphysical qualities mimic that of jasper, helping with the root chakra energy center, the legs, hips and lower spine. Also, assists with relaxation and quieting of the nerves. The new stone also promotes creativity and is beneficial for artists, musicians and writers because it helps to open the mind and removed blockages caused by ego. One of many new stones for the New Age, 2012 and beyond.

Jasper, Red – (rust) – Beautiful stone that works with blood disorders; it is connected to the root chakra energy center. Helps with relaxation and is a mothering stone. Helps to remove blockages from Root chakra, especially those caused or impacted by love and relationships. 2012 use is enhanced to include working through karma with soul mates.

Jasper, Rainforest – see *Rhyolite*

Jasper, Green – see *Bloodstone*

Jasper, Mook – See *Mookite*

Jet (black) – A form of petrified wood, Jet is a protector of the weak, defender of the defenseless, and stands for honor, decency, and purity of heart. Excellent tool for those who suffer from unabated fear because it is very grounding. Known for its use as a stone that protects travelers, or a traveler's amulet and also as an amulet to protect against psychic vampirism.

Kansas Pop Rocks – See Boji™ Stones

Kunzite - Pink to Lilac in color, Kunzite promotes emotional balance, inner love, friendliness, and self-discipline; helps open our sensitivity center. In 2012 and beyond, Kunzite is becoming more and more in use as a muscle relaxer and healer. When held in place over an aching muscle, Kunzite's energy radiates a healing warmth. Hematite recharges its healing energies. Kunzite is the pink variety of Spodumene, a lithium aluminum silicate. See *Hiddenite* and *Spodumene.*

Kyanite - (blue with white blading) channeling, altered states, vivid dreams, clear visualization; aligns charkas, repels negativity. Does not absorb negativity. Can be found in blue, black and rare green. 2012 and thereafter increases the healing properties of Kyanite and adds power to its energies. Kyanite is a protector of Light, and reduces negative energies brought about by dark sources. Kyanite will be front and center of homes, over doorways, windows, on the dashboards of vehicles to propel positivity forward. *Word of Caution: May contain traces of aluminum which is toxic. Do not add to drinking water. Use as etheric elixir.*

Labradorite – (opalescent gray) reduces insomnia, lessens negativity, strengthens one's sense of self-worth and enhances psychic abilities. Helps to quiet mind chatter by permitting focus; excellent tool for meditation. This stone promotes healing and love of self. It resonates with Leo, Sagittarius and Scorpio folks. The visible colors in Labradorite are referred to as 'flash' or 'labradorescence' which expresses the metaphysical meaning, as well. The 'Labradorescence" flashes in pink, blue, yellow, purple and green depending upon the angle of view and promotes 'flashes' of wisdom, inner vision and dream experiences that enhance us spiritually ~ flashes of light in the darkness to light our way. *Word of Caution: May contain traces of aluminum which is toxic. Do not add to drinking water. Use as etheric elixir.*

Lapis Lazuli – (rich, dark blue) aka *Lazurite,* opens one to psychic experiences; taps into our inner power and purifies soul and thoughts. Lapis is a harmony stone and promotes clarity of intention with others. Use Lapis to tap into your inner wisdom and connect with the Higher Self, the Universal Consciousness. Good protection stone – physically and psychically protects wearer from harm. To reap full benefits of the vibration of this stone, it should be worn against the skin. Sagittarius and Aries are often drawn to these properties. *Word of Caution: May contain traces of pyrite which is toxic. Do not add to drinking water. Use as etheric elixir.*

Larimar Stone (Caribbean blue/green) -- Tranquility to heart and soul. Soothes, uplifts, heals hurts and depression. Eliminates fear and pain of life. Stone for increasing creativity – artists' stone. Believed to be a blessing from Atlantis with Atlantean energies.

Lepidolite – (violet) promotes spiritual transcendence, cosmic awareness, emotional balance; good for insomnia; alleviates depression. Attracts good luck, drives away negativity and relieves stress. Known as the 'peace' stone. Metaphysical practitioners use Lepidolite to locate blockages in the body's energy network. Releases physical bonds and obstacles that hinder universal soul activity and movement.

Lepidocrocite – (black to red to brownish with yellow streaks) - Hydrated iron oxide that was unimpressive for its gem quality until a recent discovery in the Minas Gerais region of Brazil where it was found included in clear quartz, amethyst and smoky quartz. It contains black, needle like crystals that resemble hematite. Even though some of these minerals are microscopic and not visible within the stone, all of their properties are still within the crystal, as they are indigenous to the area where these crystals are mined. Said to assist in awakening, psychic abilities, such as telepathy, clairaudience, clairvoyance, and clairsentience.

Lodestone (rusty brown to metallic black) -- Balances yin and yang, assists in relieving confusion and emotional burdens. Magnetized hematite, draws out toxins from the body, and alleviates pain from the body's energy meridians.

Mahogany Obsidian (dark brown) – believed to remove negative psychic implants from the psyche that are set in place to hold a person back from fulfilling their life's purpose.

Malachite – (turquoise green) promotes comfort, balance, peace and sensitivity; enhances emotional maturity; purification and draws out negativity. Malachite soothes discomforts by helping to identify, recognize and release negative experiences that stand in the way of our forward growth. Has often been used as a stone of abundance, enhancing our own abilities to attract prosperity and reach set goals. *Word of Caution: May contain traces of copper which is toxic. Do not add to drinking water. Use as etheric elixir.*

Marcasite (silver, metallic) – This is a stone for grounding. Improves mental clarity, helps improve memory and focus. Wonderful tool for calming and settling an anxious heart. Helps to instill will power, confidence and a sense of endurance that carries forward to the physical. *Word of Caution: Contains mercury and a high concentration of iron which are toxic. Do not add to drinking water. Use as an etheric elixir.*

Moldavite - Strengthens and enhances inner journeys, channeling, cosmic consciousness, communication with interdimensional, extraterrestrial and interterrestrial forces. Genuine Moldavite is found only in the Moldau Valley of Czechoslovakia. Excellent stone for anyone seeking to enrich their connection to crystals, stones, rocks and elemental tools; however, its energies are said to be very powerful. Be prepared for sudden shifts in vibrational levels between wearer and grounding energies of the Earth. 2012 activation brings this stone onboard as an interdimensional beacon for communication between human life sources, plant life sources and alien life sources.

Interesting feature of Moldavite (and Tektite, too) is that in order to really 'hear' its message, one must tilt their head to the side slightly. This is because extraterrestrial stones (of which Moldavite is one), are aligned with Pineal Gland activation – both uploads and downloads – for DNA modifications 2012 and beyond. *Word of Caution: May contain traces of aluminum which is toxic. Do not add to drinking water. Use as etheric elixir.*

Mookite – (yellow, brown, red, orange) – stone of stabilization, Mookite (also known as *Mookaite, Mook-Mook,* and *Mook Jasper*), it is said to enable the wearer to be receptive to change and to live in the 'now' rather than dwell in the past. Balances inner and outer selves. A protector stone that enhances courage, endurance, and inner strength.

Moonstone – (white to gray to brown) promotes good fortune, nurturing, mothering, unselfishness, happiness, humanitarian love, and spiritual insight. Stone of femininity, helps wearer to connect with their feminine side. Good stone for those who travel or work on or near water. Protector during childbirth and pregnancy. Brings out love and helps love to develop to its fullest potential. Moonstone also promotes the healing process after surgery or invasive medical procedures. *Word of Caution: May contain traces of aluminum which is toxic. Do not add to drinking water. Use as etheric elixir.*

Moqui Marbles (silver-silver) - Used for shamanic journeys, psychic journeys and astral travel. Strengthens psychic power and lessens unwanted psychic influences. If you are fortunate enough to find one, you will be blessed with the incredible energies and balancing forces that Moqui Marbles contain. Protects against psychic attacks, and other unbalancing forces. Physically benefits the veins, arteries, muscles and immune system.

Moqui Marbles are thought to have been naturally formed upon meteorite impact into sand and are literally 'splash' drops of hematic-coated sand and iron. They weather-out of the Navajo Sandstone in and around south-central and south-eastern Utah, northern Arizona and north-western Colorado. This iron oxide concretion is rare and no longer being mined, per se; although, it can still be discovered in the wild due to weathering.

Word of Note: The majority of lands where Moqui Marbles exist are federal lands, Native lands or privately owned properties. All forms of collecting are prohibited on federal lands and one should seek permission before trespassing on private or Native properties.

Morganite (Pink Beryl) – inspiration, love, empathy and patience. Stone for spirituality. Works with heart chakra energy center. Carries a very high vibration frequency. Said to be the perfect stone to enact contact with Angel entities and contains one of the highest and purest frequencies for Angel connection.

Mother of Pearl – efficiency, house cleaning, nurturing. Good for men who are single parents. Said to be a stone of protection for children. Although not technically a stone, Mother of Pearl is the iridescent inner lining of the mussel shell where pearls grow. Believed by ancients to improve the luster of skin, it is also believed to help with healing of wounds and injured sites.

Mugglestone (gray and rust) -- Also known as 'Tiger Iron" and Stromatolite, this stone is believed to alleviate pain in the body, helps with follow through. A combination of hematite, red jasper and tiger's eye, this is a grounding stone that protects the wearer from potential danger. Related to sacral and root chakras. 2012 activation brings about powerful healing energies for root and sacral energy centers, removing sluggishness and blockages; healing to central nervous system of the body in harmonics with DNA modifications.

Obsidian (black) – improves immunity, useful for scrying, acts as a psychic mirror. Helpful in shamanic ceremonies, transmutes energies into white light. One of the first stones to be used in tool making because of its ability to maintain a sharp edge, Obsidian carries powerful energy and so is considered a warrior's stone. Use Obsidian to discover your inner strength, for self-empowerment and to cut away old patterns that no longer serve a purpose in your life.

Obsidian – Snowflake – (black with white splotches). Carries strong energy, but is delivered in a more gentle manner. Excellent for constipation, both physical and emotional (remember – As above, So below!). Helps to loosen old patterns and remove them. Opens the energy system and keeps it free flowing. Very useful tool for Lightworkers.

Onyx - (black) increases stamina, vigor and strength; enables grounding. Stone of determination and steadfastness, it is helpful in letting go of the past and things that no longer serve purpose in your life. Onyx absorbs energy and is useful for tapping into the Universal Life Force for channeling elsewhere where needed in your life. Also good for absorbing negative energy of others, deflecting it away from you. Strengthening stone for those born under the sign of Leo.

Opal – (white with fiery brilliance) love, loyalty, peace, faithfulness. Emotional stone that reflects the mood of the wearer. 2012 activates Opal as a grounding stone, useful to balance creative energies in those folk who tend to scatter their energies, rather than channel them for their higher purpose.

Orange Millennium™ - Another new mineral find for the 21st Century. Calms the survivor fears of the lower four chakras; a stone for balancing; lessens fears of isolation, being alone, vulnerability to attack, loss, powerlessness. Treats deep rooted fears and enables a sense calm in any storm. Calms the digestive tract and promotes the feeling of inner safety and a deep sense of belonging to the Earth. Orange Millennium™ is a natural form of Carnelian Nodules, a round-ish shaped stone that is found only in the high desert region of the United States. This stone is very important as we face the oncoming changes posed by the 2012 alignment. For those who have fear, this stone quells the root causes of victim consciousness; for those who fear change, this stone bolsters courage and purpose.

Orange Millennium™ is the stone for the New Age – small, compact, yet incredibly powerful. Carry three small stones with you every day, in your pocket, purse, or place them in your clothing against your body for full impact. Larry Coyote wrote " ... relief is brought by the knowingness that you are a child of the Earth and are connected to her core; you are here to witness the Earth changes and be changed by them; and that you are safe going through these changes if you let it be safe."

Peacock Ore – see Chalcopyrite

Pearl - although not a mineral per se, the pearl is said to bring about the matrix of the living sea, layer by layer. Enhances focus, peace and serene energy. Pearl is a gift of love, representing purity of intent. If you have issues with negative intent, carry Pearl in your pocket to help strengthen your resolve.

Pecos Diamond – (Peach colored) Pretty silica quartz stone encased within gypsum and found in the Pecos River Valley in the southeastern New Mexico and western Texas region only. Promotes love and helps one to discover their true life's path; stabilizes emotions. This stone has a very soft and gentle energy that helps to calm anxieties caused by fear of lack or loss.

Peridot – (lt. green) A powerful stone of rebirth and renewal; enhances healing of relationships, lessens anger and jealousy. The 2012 activations bring Peridot on board to promote healing the past and infusing trust into one's now.

Petrified Wood (browns, reds) – Incredible stone that formed hundreds of thousands of years ago and which retains the look and shape of the original structure, albeit crystallized as quartz or silicate. A point in history, a tree or forest of trees became buried under perhaps hundreds of feet of lava and ash, which sealed off oxygen and halted decomposition of the wood fibers. Water filtered down through the ash, bringing with it mineralized silica sand from the surface. The silica replaced the wood fibers over time, resulting in petrifaction.

Depending upon the elements above the buried forest, the colors of the resultant petrified wood will vary from black, to green, blue, red, brown, yellow, pink, orange or white.

Metaphysical properties are varied. Petrified Wood helps to eliminate worries. This is an excellent stone for new beginnings. It works with the hearing impaired and those who suffer from incontinence. A grounding and stabilizing stone, the activations of 2012 bring Petrified Wood to the elevation where it can and will facilitate healing of brain dysfunction, Alzheimer's Syndrome, Senile Dementia and certain spinal cord injuries.

Pipestone - (soft red, rust, brown) traditional stone used in Native American ceremonies, for making totems and pipes. Also known as *Catlinite*, it is used as a grounding stone for prayers and ritual. Used to connect with the spirit world.

Puddingstone (white with red spots) – Also known as Jasper Conglomerate, this stone is actually a red jasper in white quartzite. Interesting stone that is believed to protect one from spells. Negativity is said to be unable to penetrate it. Said to have supernatural powers and is a good stone for protection. 2012 and Beyond will see Puddingstone coming into its own right as a healer for those who suffer from blood disorders and circulatory problems.

Pyrite –(Fool's Gold) intellectually stimulating, stabilizes the mind, links the left and right brain hemispheres and unionizes logic and emotions. Believed to help heal the body and repel germs that cause colds, flu and infection when worn on the body. *Word of Caution: Contains traces of sulphur which is toxic. Do not add to drinking water. Use as etheric elixir.*

Quartz (also known as "Crystals") - most versatile mineral in a metaphysical sense; alignment of all chakras. Enhances, strengthens healing, cleanses mind and spirit, amplifies energies and use of other stones. Color range is from transparent, to smoky to milky and oftentimes can be as clear as glass. Clear Quartz is the most sought after and most powerful healing and energy amplifier on earth. See Chapters 7 and 8 for in depth crystal information.

Red Sandstone (rust colored) Rock most noted at Sedona, Arizona and along the Mogollon Rim south of Flagstaff. There are psychic energies in Sedona Sandstone that emanate from over 350 million years of absorbing experiences. This is a stone of records that holds the key to physical life. Useful during meditation to tap into past life experiences.

2012 use is very powerful for contact with past selves, to 'meet yourself' in dream state. Metaphysical use for 2012 and beyond is healing from a deeper level, adjusting DNA and getting physical bodies adjusted to DNA changes. Multidimensional healing. Contains essence of vortex energies for increased mind, body, and spirit connection.

Rhodochrosite - (pink sapphire) smooth energy flow, offers comfort, amity, friendship' soothing to the heart, stimulates love and compassion; promotes intuitive responses. Believed to increase fertility and to protect reproductive organs. *Word of Caution: May contain traces of lead which is toxic. Do not add to drinking water. Use as etheric elixir.*

Rhodizite – (creamy white) – Powerful stone from Russia that is one of the numerous hi-lights of the 2012 stone activations. A very powerful chakra enhancer, Rhodizite is charged with clearing, cleansing and supporting the seven existing energy centers and bringing on board the fourteen new chakra energy centers above the Crown. This stone is considered to be a Master Crystal and also one of the top five healing crystals, up there with Amethyst,

Quartz, Obsidian and Selenite. Rhodizite likes to work in sets of three, and is related to the Solar Plexus. Place Rhodizite in a natural fiber bag and wear it around your neck so that it hangs close to Solar Plexus. You can also wire wrap tiny Rhodizite crystals with sterling silver to wear around your neck for spiritual and physical protection.

Rhodizite empowers other crystals and stones, amplifying the energies, properties and metaphysical benefits of any stone in which it comes into contact. It is also beneficial as a psychic's tool, enhancing visions, remote viewing, and the clair senses.

Excellent healing qualities for emotional, psychic and physical maladies. There are energy workers who swear that Rhodizite cures dis-ease and that it has been known to cause spontaneous healing. I have not witnessed this type of healing, but can definitely attest to the power in these tiny little stones. They are of a very high vibration and when held in my hand, I became acutely aware of a tingling sensation and warmth – and from such tiny little stones! Amazing.

In 2012 and beyond, we will be hearing more and more about these wonderful stones as metaphysical tools. Cancer, diabetes, high blood pressure, and other modern dis-eases will fade into the past as we become accustomed to crystal healing. Rhodizite was used in our past, on Atlantis and by the Lemurians and it is gearing up to take its rightful place in our Now.

Rhodonite (pink with black) – This is a self-confidence stone, and aids in grace and beauty. Promotes inner growth and heals old hurts and relationships. Instrumental in locating true love. Used to balance the psychic centers, Rhodonite affects the whole being by raising the vibratory rate of the user to 528 hertz, the love frequency.

Rhyolite – (Green) – aka *Rainforest Jasper*. Stone of incredible beauty, often with brightly colored swirls and patterning in yellows, pinks, purple, reds and browns. This is a 'pet psychic' stone, opening the communication pathway between human and pet friend, especially felines. Helps to strengthen the bond between pets and humans, particularly children. 2012 activation elevates Rhyolite as a stone of release that works with our inner child, bringing peace and harmony. Increases one's ability to channel totem animal and elemental wisdom.

Richterite (Blue found with Sugalite) - Stone for meditation, contemplation, communion and peace. Helps to release the need to conquer, control, build and amass. Stone of unification. 2012 enhancements to Richterite make it most useful for those placed in positions of power. The biggest impact of 2012 is the ability for Richterite to maintain balance and effectiveness while giving the user strength in working from a place of love for the good of the whole. Richterite, although considered rare, is found in Sweden; Quebec, Canada; Myanmar; Madagascar; and in the Leucite Hills area of Wyoming. Interestingly, it has been located in Canyon Diablo, Arizona, the site of a meteorite crater.

River Rock – (brown, black, gray) – aggregate stones washed smooth by Mother Nature. These are the teaching stones, stones of patience, of empathy and of endurance. River Rock makes a good 'worry stone' because they are smooth and rubbing them enhances their energies. River Rock emerges as a stone of strength in 2012 and beyond not only because they are good teachers but because they are good listeners, as well. Often times, this is a stone that asks to be moved or tossed, and loves movement.

Rose Quartz – (Pale Pink) - enhances love, forgiveness, self-forgiveness, and compassion; diminishes fear, anger, resentment, addictions. Helps with weightloss. 2012 activation charges this stone as a very powerful healing remedy used in elixirs, tinctures and as an etheric specialist. Rose Quartz vibrates at a frequency that resonates organically within the body. This vibration causes deeper healing, clearing, adjusting and rapidly causes the creation of new, healthy cells.

Ruby – (Red corundrum) happiness, healing, devotion, courage; balances blood sugar, improves energy after exhaustion; aids in vitality, energy, stamina and endurance. Strengthens physical stability. Enhancements from 2012 activation include strengthening of root chakra and kundalini expansion. *Word of Caution: May contain traces of aluminum which is toxic. Do not add to drinking water. Use as etheric elixir.*

Rutilated Quartz (clear to brown with inclusions of hair-like 'rutiles') – Angel stone that heals and promotes aura balance; helps to get to the 'root' of a problem. Strengthens blood vessels and circulatory system. Repels unwanted interference from physical and spiritual planes. Believed to relieve loneliness, rutiliated quartz attracts love and is thought to stabilize relationships. An enhancer of creativity, it helps to assist in important decision making, by giving the wearer the power to make the right choices that will improve business and increase wealth building. A good crystal for those in business. Also believed to slow the aging process and aid in cellular regeneration. Maintains a protective shield around wearer that deflects negative energies.

Sapphire - (blue) increases hope, faith, intelligence, wisdom, prophecy and happiness. Blue, green, pink, purple and clear stones. Helps pituitary gland and thyroid gland. Aids in detoxing the body. Stops nosebleeds. Symbol of heaven and often called the "Stone of Destiny" because it improves ones spiritual perception and devotion to God the Creator. *Word of Caution: May contain traces of aluminum which is toxic. Do not add to drinking water. Use as etheric elixir.*

Sardonynx - (black, green) - favors luck, friendship, happiness and good fortune; a gambler's stone. Stone of strength and protection enhances willpower, integrity, stamina and vigor. Also good stone for marriages. Used in grids to protect home.

Selenite - (clear) Sometimes referred to as Gypsum, this is a higher planes attunement stone that works with the universal consciousness, and brings mental clarity and acuity. Helps to attune to Angelic realm for guidance and communication. Selenite works with the subtle body that connects the physical self to the higher self.

This is a delicate stone that is easily scratched or broken; however, it is also easy to work with, shape and carve. The physical properties of selenite make it all the more powerful in metaphysical applications. The vibration of selenite is extremely high making it an excellent stone for meditation. Its use in 2012 and beyond is to raise the vibratory rate of the user to increase the ability of telepathic communication and auditory contact with ethereal and interdimensional beings.

Selenite is sometimes referred to as moon rock, or moon stone because of its ability to disperse light through its pearly luster. Clear selenite has a glow about it that is both ethereal and mystical.

Selenite, Blue is used for meditation because of its ability to quiet the mind and settle the anxious 'chatter' that oftentimes disrupts quite moments.

Selenite, Brown is a grounding tool that works with the higher self in manifesting desires in the physical.

Selenite, Green is a healing tool that is useful in drawing off joint pain and aches associated with the aging process.

Selenite, Desert Rose is a beautiful cluster of clear gypsum and sand, used by healing practitioners to align the spine and to pull chakras into alignment. Strong stone for those who suffer from brain disorders and seizures.

Septarian (Dragonstone) – (swirled mix of yellow, brown and white) Healing stone that benefits the triad – body, mind and spirit. Opens psychic abilities while nurturing and grounding the wearer. Clears blockages of Root Chakra Energy Center.

Serpentine (chartreuse jade) - offers protection against poisonous elements such as snakes, insects and vegetation. Promotes peace in conflict. Helpful for stomach and menstrual cramping.

Seraphenite – (green and white) - used to connect with Angelic Realm, offers greater awareness of the Divine Feminine; restores health and balance.

Shattuckite - blue and green - Stone of protection, aids against psychic attacks and negative influences. This stone has a high vibratory rate, so it enhances every thought we think. When you hold Shattuckite, think loving, positive thoughts to attract pure spirits and high level guides. 2012 activation enhances the metaphysical qualities of attraction to develop further psychic visions and interdimensional communication.

Silver - hope, unconditional, universal love. Moon Goddess and reflects Goddess' attributes of mothering, nurturance, gentle strength.

Smoky Quartz – dusky clear from brown to dark brown – This quartz promotes calmness, realism, grounding, and stability. Stone for those working with patience because it works slowly and steadily and the energy remains for a longer period of time after you have used it. Great stone to create etherically because it continues to work long after its visage dissipates. Excellent stone to promote teamwork. 2012 activation enhances this stone's metaphysical properties to act as a negativity release, especially in relationships, both personal and business.

Snow Quartz– (white) – promote good luck and relieves stress. Stone of innocence, protector of children and inner child in adults. 2012 activation adds healing to this stone's repertoire — it can draw out infection, abscesses, boils, and toxins from the body. Can be used etherically or in the physical.

Soapstone — see Steatite

Sodalite — (blue w/white) empowers logical thinking, intelligence, emotional balance; promotes healing of thyroid problems and is a good stone for diabetics. Increase courage, endurance and removes guilt and fear. Brings inner peace to wearer. Good writer's stone as it promotes creativity and unlocks writer's block.

Sodalite is a beautiful azure blue stone drizzled with bright white. It is an igneous rock of volcanic origin that is chemically composed of sodium, aluminum, silicon, chlorine and oxygen. Sodalite does not carry radiation.

The healing powers of Sodalite work with the Throat Chakra Energy Center. It is a stone of communication, self-expression and aids in clarity of thought before words are spoken. This is a stone for public speakers and those who work in the arts where using their voice is necessary. A good stone for singers, as well, since Sodalite protects the throat, vocal chords, neck, mouth, and auditory organs.

It is said that Sodalite has the property to draw off infections in the head and neck area, and helps to sooth sinus, tooth, and neuralgia pain.

In the body, Sodalite affects the thyroid and pituitary glands, and aids the lymphatic system in releasing toxins dislodged by clearing and balancing work. It is also said that this mineral strengthens the metabolism. Sodalite works well when used with Citrine to aid digestion and is helpful in the treatment of digestive disorders. Because of its impact on the body's glandular system, it is also believed that Sodalite assists the pancreas and liver in regulating blood sugar making this a beneficial stone for those with diabetes or at risk.

And, like its relative, Lapis Lazuli, Sodalite helps to eliminate confusion, bring clarity and facilitates spiritual growth.

Besides all these wonderful metaphysical properties, Sodalite is a beautiful stone to add to your metaphysical toolbox or jewelry wardrobe. *Word of Caution: May contain traces of aluminum which is toxic. Do not add to drinking water. Use as etheric elixir.*

Spinel - range of colors, pinks, reds, blues, greens, purples, but most often found as red - Beautiful gem stone of protection, used in the past to protect the wearer from harm. When given as a gift, Spinel is believed to hold the giver's love within it. 2012 activation brings Spinel online as a healer for the heart chakra center and enhances its loving qualities of peace, gentility and serenity. *Word of Caution: May contain traces of aluminum and zinc which are toxic. Do not add to drinking water. Use as etheric elixir.*

Spodumene (translucent gray to water clear) – A major source of lithium used in batteries and anti-depressants among other modern day uses. Spodumene is associated with the astrological sign of Scorpio. 2012 and beyond will find spodumene coming into the spotlight to help with ascension by bringing forward those who have been quiet for too long a time. As the phoenix rose from the ashes, so shall those who use spodumene to strengthen their resolve. A tool for ascension, spodumene vibrates at a very high frequency and raises the frequency of the user. Removes negativity and acts as a protector stone. Excellent to help achieve a meditative state easily. See Hiddenite and Kunzite.

Steatite – Steatite has been used in slab form as a carving source for many things. Because it absorbs heat, it is useful as a radiant source. Metaphysically in 2012 and thereafter, Steatite (aka Soapstone) will capitalize on this absorption quality, allowing the user to take in universal life force energy and distribute it to others as necessary. Great stone for healers, light and energy workers. Helpful in accepting and working with change. Excellent for opening the pathways through the dimensions.

Stibnite – (silver) unusual sharded stone; stone of transformation, great wealth and power. Helps one to expand their outlook and perception, and to achieve goals. *Word of Caution: Contains traces of lead and antimony which are toxic and transferable to skin. Do not add to drinking water. Use as etheric elixir.*

Stromatolite – See Mugglestone. Also known as Tiger Iron.

Sugilite – (lavender, violet) a healer's stone, enhances ability to heal, strengthens spirituality, psychic connection, channeling. Increases love and wisdom. This stone is being elevated to the Ascension path during the 2012 activations and thereafter as the stone of forgiveness of self and others. Sugilite has a very powerful healing energy that will be increased and enhanced to be used to heal ailments of all kinds from sinus infections to kidney stones to arthritis pain. Stone works on the central nervous system and will help to alleviate neuropathy and neuropathic pain disorders.

Sunstone - (pink, orange, red, brown) - This stone is also known as 'aventurine feldspar' and is found in Canada, Russia, Norway, Tanzania and Australia; Oregon, Virginia, North Carolina, New York State, Maine, Arkansas, New Jersey, Pennsylvania and South Carolina in the United States. A form of feldspar, Sunstone is said to harness the power of the sun, offering comfort and protection. Gives courage to the wearer/user, enabling one to show outstanding bravery in the face of fear. This is an excellent stone for soldiers, law enforcement and paramilitary constituents or any one facing life-challenging fear.

Sunstones (Oregon) – (clear pale yellow, orange, red) – A variety of 'aventurine feldspar' or "Sunstone", this stone is found mainly in Lake and Harney counties in Oregon's central core. Volcanic in origin, this is a strong stone of protection which increases the power of personal attraction. Acts much like quartz in that it is a powerfully harmonic frequency stimulator. Promotes energy transmissions. Stone of the New Age, Sunstones will ascend to their rightful place in 2012 and thereafter as a harmonic facilitator.

Super Seven Crystal - This stone is comprised of seven components - Amethyst, Clear Quartz, Smoky Quartz, Cacoxenite, Rutile, Goethite and Lepidocrocite combined - and contains all the energies of the seven components. This combination of stones has lead to the name *"Super Seven."* And is also known as *"Melody's Stone,"* named after the internationally known author and crystal practitioner. *Super Seven* was discovered in Brazil in the Espirito do Santo region of Minas Gerais, an area which is known for its many varieties of included quartz and other gemstone crystals. *See Chapter - Crystal Formations and Metaphysical Meaning*

Tanzanite - (blue - purple) A variety of Zoisite, this beauteous stone is found in the foothills of Mt. Kilamanjaro in Tanzania. This stone begins as a reddish-brown stone and is transformed into the stunning bluish-purple gem after being heated in a jeweler's oven. Originally known as 'blue zoisite', it was renamed "tanzanite" after a marketing campaign by Tiffany & Co. to promote the world's only known location of the stone. Known to be a psychic's stone, Tanzanite enhances psychic abilities, communication with spiritual guides, and promotes mysticism. Works with brow, throat and heart chakra energy centers. Increase of metaphysical qualities in 2012 and enhancements to include protection of crystalline children; grid source protection for psychics and energy workers.

Tektite – (charcoal gray) This stone is extraterrestrial in nature and so, it supports communication and contact with extra-terrestrials; expands psychic attunement and clears lower chakras. 2012 activation brings this stone onboard as an interdimensional beacon for communication between human life sources, plant life sources and alien life sources. Interesting feature of Tektite (and Moldavite, too) is that in order to really 'hear' its message, one must tilt their head to the side slightly. This is because Tektite is aligned with Pineal Gland activation – both uploads and downloads – for DNA modifications 2012 and beyond. *Word of Caution: May contain traces of aluminum or other metals which are toxic. Do not add to drinking water. Use as etheric elixir.*

Thulite (pink) – aka Pink Zoisite, is a stone known to help those who cannot see their own beauty. It is a stone of self-love, helping the user/wearer to more clearly see themselves for who they are, a child of the Universe, a spark of the Divine. This is a teaching stone, gently teaching lessons of love, life and harmony.

Tibetan Quartz – (clear, sometimes 'Tourmalinated'- *see Tourmalinated Quartz*) Tibetan quartz is said to be the most resilient of the healing quartz stones. Believed to carry the "Om" frequency and vibration, Tibetan Quartz radiates a higher healing resonance that directly correlates to the Higher Self. Holding a Tibetan Crystal in ones' hand and visualizing the alignment of the body's energy centers make it so because these crystals contain the entire color healing spectrum.

Tiger's Eye - (yellowish-brown) also called "Cat's Eye" - improves clear thinking process, personal empowerment, will power; useful to 'see' things from a different, more clear perspective. Offers discernment. Brings good luck and fortune. Enhancements for 2012 bring with it increased qualities of inner vision and dream travel.

Tiger Iron - Combination of red jasper, hematite and tiger's eye, also known as Stromatolite – see "Mugglestone" above.

Topaz – (blue, yellow, brown) - self-confidence, optimism, creativity, abundance. Empowering energies, heals and soothes. Helps to rid bad habits, draws love and improves charisma of the wearer. Said to stimulate the appetite. 2012 enhancement to bring strength to the weak of spirit, and to improve the users abilities to stand in their own empowerment.

Tourmaline – (black, green, pink) Gem tourmalines were discovered in Sri Lanka by the Dutch East India Company and brought to Europe in large quantities. Aka Schorl, black tourmaline is found in a number of places worldwide. The black variety of Tourmaline enhances happiness, serenity, and positive transformation; opens Heart Chakra. The green variety is used as a good luck stone. The pink variety enhances the ability to love. Its been said that to rub a black Tourmaline stone is to increase one's good luck.

The Dravite variety of Tourmaline comes from the Drava river area of Europe. Elbaite Tourmaline comes from Elba Island, Italy. Dravite and Elbaite are uncommon varieties and quite rare; however, both Dravite and Elbaite carry potent energies of Tourmaline and are wonderful additions to your Metaphysical Toolbox.

Tourmaline today is found across the globe in the United States and Canada, Brazil, Africa, Pakistan, Sri Lanka, and Afghanistan.

Tourmalinated Quartz – (clear w/black inclusions) Quartz amplifies Tourmaline's harmonic resonance. Tourmalinated Quartz is very special ~~ a powerful protector. Depending upon intent, it can either amplify energy and return it to the wearer, or repel negative energies placed in the direction of the wearer. Either way, this stone has been used through the ages to balance energies and release negative patterns. Usually, Black Tourmalinated Quartz comes to us at a time in our lives when we are ready to release pain from the past and eliminate the hold that negativity has tried to keep on us. *See Tibetan Quartz*

Turquoise - protection, balance strength, energy, wisdom, and friendship. Empathic stone, teaches empathy for others to the wearer' protects against negativity of others. Is a cherished symbol of enduring friendship.. Enhancements for 2012 and thereafter bring Turquoise full circle as a stone that disseminates ancient wisdom to seekers with pure intent. *Word of Caution: May contain traces of copper which is toxic. Do not add to drinking water. Use as etheric elixir.*

Ulexite – (clear to opaque white) aka "TV Stone." It is composed of closely packed fibrous crystals that have a fiber-optic quality which transmit light along its length by internal reflection. Ulexite, when polished, displays the reflection of whatever surface is adjacent to its other side.

Ulexite is a Lightworkers' stone. It is known to promote emotional, mental, psychic and spiritual clarity.

Ulexite will become a very powerful tool for 2012 and beyond because it acts as a fiber-optic conductor between user and Source. Today, we use Ulexite as a stone for resolution to amplify our being able to see clearly to discover purpose; tomorrow we will use it as a spiritual magnifying glass that enhances all that we see, so we may truly see the root of all things and resolutions to any further obstacles. Very powerful, yet has remained mostly an unknown tool. Ulexite's time is here.

Ulexite is a very soft stone, and will dissolve in hot water.

Unakite (green – pink) -- aka Epidote or Epidotized Granite. This is a stone that stands for rebirth and growth; helps release hindrances that inhibit growth. Excellent for weight gain and recuperation after illness. Unakite is a miracle stone and has the power to make wishes come true.

Variscite – (green) -- Stress stone, excellent assistant for those whose job creates stress because it helps to bring the physical body in tune with the spiritual bodies and promote balance, equilibrium. *Word of Caution: May contain traces of aluminum which is toxic. Do not add to drinking water. Use as etheric elixir.*

Vogel Cut Quartz Crystals – natural quartz crystals with a specific faceted cut as created by Dr. Marcel Vogel, retired IBM research scientist whose love of crystals powered his metaphysical research after he retired. Dr. Vogel knew that natural crystal was the most powerful amplifier that could cohere and transmit frequencies; however, he found that in its natural state, crystal did not transmit healing energies sufficiently.

So, he began to experiment with cutting and discovered that the amplification of the crystals energies were greatly enhanced by the side-facetings cut into the crystal. He started with 4-sided faceting and increased with different numbers of facets: 6, 8, 11, 12, 13, 21, 24, 33 and Dream Cuts.

> *"The crystal is a neutral object whose inner structure exhibits a state of perfection and balance. When it's cut to the proper form and when the human mind enters into relationship with its structural perfection, the crystal emits a vibration which extends and amplifies the power of the user's mind. Like a laser, it radiates energy in a coherent, highly concentrated form, and this energy may be transmitted into objects or people at will."*
>
> -- Marcel Vogel

Wulfenite - Orange, Red - Stone of harmony that integrates and aligns the lower chakras. Excellent stone to remove blockages of the lower chakras, and is soothing to lower back. 2012 enhancements bring Wulfenite on board as a healer of the lower extremities, sexual organs, sacral and solar plexus region. *Word of Caution: Contains traces of lead and molybdenum which are toxic. Do not add to drinking water. Use as etheric elixir.*

Zincite – Stone of many colors ~ green, yellow, orange, red ~ and most often man-made. Naturally occurring Zincite is very rate. Most of what is available is created as a by-product of zinc smelting and found crystallized in the smokestacks. Small grain, natural Zincite has been found in New Jersey and in Italy.

Whether you have the small, naturally occurring crystals or the man-made by-product of zinc smelting, Zincite is a very powerful stone. 2012 and beyond elevates Zincite to the positive aspects of ascension, being used to keep us grounded while in the third dimension. Zincite readies the body for physical ascension and the spirit for spiritual ascension quickly by affecting the lower chakras, opening and clearing them. When you hold Zincite in your hand, be prepared for immediate vibratory enhancement and frequency lift. Best used in small doses to allow the spiritual bodies to get used to the energy. *Word of Caution: May contain traces of zinc which is toxic. Do not add to drinking water. Use as etheric elixir.*

Zircon (multiple colors) -- symbolic of purity, clarity, innocence. Known to pull all bodies together – spiritual, physical, emotional, psychic and mental bodies; connects to the higher realms. Offers strength of purpose to the wearer.

Zoisite (pink, green) - Beautiful stone used to establish and solidify trust in the process of life. Helps to release fears and allow user to work from a place of love and trust. 2012 activations enhance these qualities and additionally dissipates fear by increasing light. This is a stone of vitality, love, joy and light that strengthens resolve and opens the door to effect resolution and peace.

ALPHABETICAL GUIDE TO CRYSTALS AND STONES USE BY SYMPTOM AND ISSUE

Using rocks, crystals and stones in healing are affected by our intent. Our connection to Spirit, our pure love on the highest level and our ability to telepathically send loving energy to ourselves and others is what carries the effectiveness of the stone on its healing journey.

In our world of duality, everything is in perfect balance with both positive and negative energy. For every negative instance, there is a corresponding positive instance. If there is hot, there must be cold to act as a counteragent. This is the Spiritual Law of Balance. And so it is with the healing use of rocks, crystals and stones.

If you are treating someone for fever, which is the physical act of rising energy, your intent must be to reduce or abate the energy by using negative intent to draw off the rising energy; likewise if your intent is to reduce pain, or swelling.

Be completely clear in your negative intent and the stone or crystal will carry your intent as a deficit, to draw away the symptom, rather than to increase its energy. This sounds quite the opposite of what a light or energy worker might do in their practice; however, there are certain stone and crystal configurations that are used precisely for this purpose, to receive or draw on one end, while transmitting or giving with the other end.

If your intent is to improve or increase awareness, or to build toward positivity, the listed stones will heighten and empower your intent toward the positive.

Our intent is of the utmost important, as is our clarity of purpose. Please be clear in spirit and intent before using stones or crystals to create an action.

A good way to use the power of rocks, crystals and stones is to create an elixir. Elixirs are powerful remedies that heal and treat dis-eases and afflictions on multiple levels, physically and spiritually.

A simple way to make an elixir is to add the stone to a small bottle of water to which has been added a touch of brandy. The alcohol carries a high vibration and therefore adds to the healing frequency of the stone. Elixirs are taken by dropper so there is no danger of swallowing the stone. However, if you have concern about swallowing the stone or crystal, you may add the rock, crystal or stone etherically, that is, place it in the bottle with your mind's eye. Visualize the stone in the bottle and repeat its name three times to punctuate its presence. This empowers the energies of the stone etherically causing the brandy/water mixture to become a potent and powerful elixir.

This guide will help you to choose the correct stone or crystal for the corresponding symptom. Each symptom below represents an ailment or issue. The stones listed are traditionally used for healing. You may place the stone physically on the affected part of the body, or place it etherically. Both ways are powerful.

A

Abandonment: garnet, smoky quartz, thulite

Ability (tapping into): ajoite, atlantisite, smoky quartz, sodalite

Abundance: agate, green aventurine, aqua aura, bloodstone, citrine, diamond, jade, malachite, moonstone, moss agate, peridot, topaz, smoky quartz, rutilated quartz, tree agate, turquoise

Acting career: aquamarine, carnelian, fluorite, orange millennium™, rhodonite

Acceptance: danburite, dumortierite (blue quartz), bloodstone

Addictions – general – bloodstone, selenite, seraphinite, ametrine, Botswana agate, coral, citrine, green calcite, Herkimer diamond, malachite, moki marbles, rose quartz, thulite

Addictions – alcohol and drugs: amethyst (esp reduces withdrawal symptoms), coral, chevron amethyst, citrine, dumortierite, green calcite, Herkimer diamond, iolite, malachite-azurite, moki marbles, phenacite, rose quartz, rutilated quartz, sugilite (esp immune system problems from substance abuse), thulite (esp those caused by abuse/neglect)

Adrenal glands: ametrine, aventurine (green), black obsidian, tourmaline, bloodstone, carnelian, emerald, epidote, fire agate, garnet, jade, Kansas pop rocks aka Boji™ Stones, black kyanite, malachite, rose quartz, ruby, smoky quartz, sugilite

Afterlife (passage): coral, celestite, aqua aura crystal, Christ commune crystal

AIDS: andalusite, catlinite, quartz crystal, dolomite, garnet, halite, petrified wood, red jasper, rutilated quartz, Tibetan quartz crystal, tourmalinated quartz

Alignment: (Astral bodies) amazonite, chrysocolla, labrodorite, blue kyanite

Alignment: (Chakra system) – blue kyanite, bloodstone, phenacite, rhodizite, quartz crystal

Allergies: apatite, brecciated jasper (allergies to animals) carnelian, clay, dolomite, garnet, moldovite, coral

Amplification of Energies: quartz crystal, hawk's eye, Himalayan rock salt

Ancient wisdom: celestite, Lemurian crystal, quartz crystal

Anemia: bloodstone, garnet, granite, hematite

Angels (for communication): angelite, apatite, amethyst, aquamarine, blue lace agate, celestite, danburite, fulgarite, moonstone, morganite, muscovite, selenite

Anger: aquamarine, aragonite, bronzite, citrine, gold, howlite, jet, lepidolite, king cobra jasper, kunzite, kyanite, peridot, rhodonite, ruby, sea shells, sodalite, turquoise

Animal Spirit Guide (connect to): amber, leopardskin jasper, jet, eagle eye agate

Anxiety: malachite, bloodstone, dolomite, labradorite, lepidolite, azurite, lapis lazuli, richterite

Architects: ammonite, sunstone, combarbalita

Arthritis: abalone, amber, amethyst, apatite, black tourmaline, blue lace agate, Boji™ stones (Kansas pop rocks), Botswana agate, carnelian, chrysocolla, copper, dolomite, fluorite, gold, green calcite, lapis lazuli, lodestone (magnetite), malachite, petrified wood, quartz, rhodonite, ruby, sulphur, topaz

Artistic expression/creative energies: Botswana agate, blue calcite, holey stone, howlite, lapis lazuli, phantom quartz, rainbow Boji™ stone (Kansas pop rocks), rainbow quartz, rutilated quartz, watermelon tourmaline

Assertiveness: cinnabar,

Asthma: green aventurine, jade, malachite, obsidian, rutilated quartz, tiger's eye

Astral travel: ametrine, apophyllite, azurite, malachite, calcite, fluorite, honey calcite, iolite, moldavite, quartz, sapphire, rhodizite

Astrology: Boji™ stones (Kansas pop rocks), moki marbles, bornite, tektite, moldavite

Attraction (Soul Mate): geodes, herderite, orange millennium™, carnelian, rhodonite

Attunement: Herkimer diamond , kunzite

Attuning to the Earth: chrysocolla, hiddenite, hematite, silver

Aura (balancing, clearing, and cleansing): ametrine, citrine, cymophane, epidote , galaxite, iolite, labradorite, super seven stone, quartz, rutilated quartz

Awareness: howlite, herderite, kunzite, lapis lazuli, picture jasper

B

Back pain: calcite, fluorite, lodestone, obsidian

Back alignment: howlite, selenite,

Balance: alexandrite, ametrine, red jasper, blue calcite, orange millennium™, celestite, mookite, white fluorite, kunzite, kyanite, tourmaline

Balance, Yin / Yang: alunite, aragonite, tourmaline, obsidian, tiger's eye, kyanite

Beauty (inner): clear quartz, dioptase, tektite, fire agate, Herkimer diamond

Beauty (outer): silica, sodalite, apatite, angelite, celestite, selenite, amber

Bee Stings: Silica, Amber, selenite

Beginnings: petrified wood, atlantisite, Herkimer diamond

Bipolar disorder (manic depressive): lepidolite, quartz, aquamarine

Black Magic – protect against: black tourmaline, tourmalinated quartz, galena, spinel

Blockages: snowflake obsidian (hidden), danburite (energy), blue kyanite, aqua aura crystal, wulfenite

Blood pressure: bloodstone, blue calcite, chrysocolla, sodalite

Blood sugar: serpentine, sodalite, rose quartz, citrine

Blood vessels/blood/circulatory system: amber, amethyst, green aventurine, bloodstone, carnelian, chalcedony, copper, coral, dalmation jasper (purify blood), fire agate, fluorite, garnet, hematite, howlite, malachite, red jasper, ruby, sapphire, mugglestone, topaz

Body aches: diopside, Herkimer Diamond, Amethyst, quartz crystal, ruby, sapphire

Body odor: leopardskin jasper, magnesite, feldspar

Bones: amethyst, blue lace agate, dolomite, fluorite, howlite, malachite, petrified wood, smoky quartz

Brain: albite, amber, aragonite, chalcopyrite, clear quartz, elestial crystal, hematite, rhodizite, seraphinite, stechtite, tourmalinated quartz

Broken heart: chrysoprase, rhodonite, rose quartz, quartz crystal

Bronchial / Lung:: amber, angelite, beryl, blue calcite, blue topaz, bornite, chrysocolla, galena, larimar, malachite, morganite, opal, tigers eye

Bronchitis: gold, lodestone, rutilated quartz

Burns: gem silica, sodalite, sugalite

Business partnerships: jade, goldstone, fluorite

C

Calming/soothing: agate, amber, aventurine, blue lace agate, bronze, calcite, galena, Herkimer diamond, lepidolite, opal, richterite, rose quartz, selenite, snow quartz, topaz, tourmaline.

Calming for pets: diopside, tiger's eye, moonstone

Cancer: azurite-malachite, fluorite, gold, hematite, holey stone, lapis, lepidolite, moonstone, red jasper, rhodocrosite, rose chalcedony, sapphire, sugilite, tourmaline

Cardiovascular: bloodstone, hematite, red jasper

Celiac Disease: tiger's eye, Oregon sun stone, variscite

Centering/grounding: bloodstone, calcite, Herkimer diamond, hematite, kunzite, onyx. *See Grounding.*

Chakra, Root: bloodstone, coral, dragonstone, ruby, obsidian, onyx, garnet, sardonyx, tiger iron, red jasper, tourmalinated quartz

Chakra, Sacral: carnelian, jasper, moonstone, orange millenium™, red calcite

Chakra, Solar Plexus: amber, citrine, yellow topaz, sunstone

Chakra, Heart: emerald, green aventurine, malachite, fuschite, serpentine, rose quartz, ruby kunzite

Chakra, Throat: apatite, aquamarine, blue quartz, chalcedony, sapphire, sodalite

Chakra, Brow: tanzanite, amethyst, azurite, charoite, lepidolite,

Chakra, Crown: clear quartz, rose quartz, opal, diamond, selenite, tourmalinated quartz

Changes / adaptability: bloodstone, Botswana agate, chiastolite, datolite, honey calcite, opal

Channeling: apophyllite, blue calcite, peacock ore, copper, moldavite, meteorites, moqui marbles, kyanite, quartz, yellow calcite

Chaos – eliminate: bustamite, cacoxenite, super seven stone, stichtite

Charity: dolomite, coral, aventurine

Childbirth: ammonite, chrysocolla (especially for preventing miscarriage), geodes, hematite, lepidolite, malachite, rose quartz

Children: chrysoprase, diopside, hematite, Botswana agate

Choices/alternatives: rhodonite, labradorite, alexandrite

Chronic fatigue: amethyst, aquamarine, aragonite, Boji™ stones (kansas pop rocks), orange calcite, quartz, rhodocrosite, ruby

Circulatory problems: puddingstone, bloodstone, rhodocrosite, rose quartz

Clairaudiance: diamond, eudialyte, Herkimer diamond, fire opal, peacock ore

Clairvoyance: ametrine, azurite-malachite, chalcopyrite (peacock ore), charoite, desautekite, diamond, emerald, green jasper, halite (salt), hematite, Herkimer diamond, kyanite, peacock ore

Clairsentience: beryl, peacock ore, quartz crystal

Clarity: amber, andalusite, danburite, diamond, dumortierite (blue quartz), tiger eye

Cleansing: amber, emerald, kyanite, tigers eye

Clearing (energetically): black tourmaline, lodestone, kyanite, meteorites, tektites

Cold sores / fever blisters: fluorite, dioptase, clear quartz

Colds common: carnelian, epidote, azeztulite

Colitis / Intestinal: cuprite, malachite, feldspar

Comfort: agate, Botswana agate, jasper, tangerine calcite

Commitment: garnet, petrified wood,

Communication: ajoite, amazonite, apatite, blue lace agate, blue onyx, hawk's eye, blue topaz, copper, emerald, euclase, kunzite, kyanite, labradorite, quartz, turquoise, ulexite

Compassion: green jasper, green tourmaline, jade, kunzite, moonstone, rose quartz, red jasper

Compatibility: green moss agate, granite, moonstone

Completion of tasks: mugglestone, red jasper

Concentration: carnelian, fluorite, jade, lapis, obsidian, quartz crystals, malachite, fluorite, goethite, hematite, ruby

Confidence: chrysocolla, jade, moonstone, rhodonite jade, moonstone,

Confusion: bloodstone, lodestone, fluorite

Contentment: red jasper, blue quartz, blue selenite

Contractors / Builders: mugglestone, smoky quartz, combarbalita

Convergence (energy): hematite, rhyolite, obsidian, quartz crystal

Counselors & therapists stone: jasper, iolite, prenhite, turquoise, serpentine

Constipation (emotional and physical): snowflake obsidian, ulexite, ametrine, citrine, unakite

Courage/ inner strength: agate, amethyst, aquamarine, aventurine, bloodstone, blue tigers eye, carnelian, charoite, chevron amethyst, chrysoprase, feldspar, fire agate, garnet, hematite, Herkimer diamond, jade, red calcite, richterite, ruby, rutile, sodalite, smoky quartz, tigers eye, tiger iron (mugglestone), variscite

Courtesy: bronzite, calcite, Herkimer diamond,

Creativity: agate, aventurine, Botswana agate, calcite, carnelian, citrine, dolomite, double terminated crystals, euclase, garnet, Herkimer diamonds, obsidian, peach aventurine, pyrite

D

Death or transition (assisting the process): amazonite, apache tears, aqua aura, jet, black quartz, Botswana agate, fossils , hematite, holey stone, malachite, obsidian, rose quartz, rainbow moonstone, tiger iron

Decision making: charoite, combarbalita, crazy lace agate, diamond, emerald, falcon's eye (blue tiger eye), fluorite, jade, tiger's eye, tourmaline

Dehydration: brecciated jasper, laramar stone, aquamarine

Denial / avoidance: rhodochrosite, malachite, quartz crystal

Depression: amber, apophylite, chrysoprase, citrine, kunzite, lepidolite, blue quartz, jet, smoky quartz, rose quartz

Detachment: green millennium™, petrified wood, chrysoberyl

Determination / resolve: tiger's eye, red jasper, blue calcite, tiger iron

Destiny (finding one's): labradorite, moonstone, danburite

Dexterity: amber, thulite, onyx

Diabetes: sodalite, cavansite, citrine

Diet/metabolism: citrine, ametrine

Digestion: blue lace agate, chrysacolla, citrine, epidote, peridot, obsidian, tigers eye, topaz

Disillusionment: dalmatian jasper, red jasper, agate

Disorientation: black tourmaline, hematite, mugglestone

Divine Feminine: amazonite, aquamarine, Lemurian star seed crystal, seraphinite, celestite, selenite, silver

Divine Masculine: gold, obsidian, tourmaline, hiddenite, fire opal

Divination: charoite, hematite, moonstone, tiger's eye

Domestic bliss: emerald, combarbalita, celestite

Dowsing: brecciated jasper, copper, lava rock

DNA Adjustment – red sandstone, Arkansas quartz crystal, ajoite, ametrine

Dreams (recall/work): Herkimer diamonds, moldavite, amethyst, rose quartz, clear quartz, citrine, jade, kyanite, labradorite, lapis lazuli, lepidolite, nebula stone, opal, prehnite, smoky quartz, ruby, tektites

E

Ears/hearing: amber, celestite, rhodonite

Eating disorders (anorexia, bulemia, others): picasso marble (jasper), thulite, ametrine, citrine, moldavite

Electrolytes: mother of pearl, seashells, coral, quartz

Emotional disturbances/trauma: amazonite, aqua aura, bloodstone, chrysocolla, citrine, diamond, dioptase, emerald, chrysoprase, jasper, labradorite, larimar, lepidolite, moonstone, peridot, rhodochrosite, rose quartz, smithsonite, thulite

Endocrine system: alexandrite, amber, amethyst, aquamarine, bloodstone, green calcite, chrysoberyl, citrine, howlite, magnetite, green obsidian, rhodochrosite, sodalite

Endurance: brecciated jasper, tanzanite, granite

Energy: amber, agate, apophyllite, aragonite (magick & charms particularly), bloodstone, blue calcite, blue goldstone, Boji™ stones (Kansas pop rocks), carnelian, clear quartz, danburite, green jasper, honey calcite, prehnite, red calcite, red coral, rhodochrosite, ruby, rutilated quartz, septarian nodule, sulphur, yellow calcite

Energy blockages/leaks: dolomite, labradorite, bornite, danburite

Enhance emotions: garnet, ruby, fuschite

Enhance energy of other crystals: tabular quartz crystal, apatite, chrysoberyl, dolomite (by balancing mineral energies), danburite, diamond, Herkimer diamonds, rhodizite, selenite

Envy: agate, green kyanite, peridot

Epilepsy: jet, lapis lazuli, tanzanite, limonite

ESP: peridot, moqui marbles, red sandstone,

Exploring the unknown: Botswana agate, moqui marbles

Extra-terrestrials (contacting): quartz crystal, cobalt, fulgarite, galaxite, herderite

Eyes/eyesight: aquamarine, celestite, charoite, green tourmaline, holey stones (eyesight in particular), labradorite, opal, rutilated quartz

F

Facing the cause of disorders: picture jasper, honey calcite

Faith: emerald, peridot, aventurine, rose quartz

Family issues: citrine, family clusters of crystals

Fear (dispel): ammonite, apatite, aquamarine, chrysacolla, chrysoprase, citrine, orange calcite, red calcite, smoky quartz, sodalite

Feet: onyx, malachite, cinnabar

Feminine reproductive-related issues: atlantisite, Botswana agate, lapis, rose quartz

Fevers: diopside, peridot, pyrite, tree agate, sapphire, sodalite

Fibromyalgia: amber, amethyst, citrine, clear quartz, emerald, hematite, lapis, labradorite, morganite, obsidian, rose quartz, tiger eye

Fidelity: jade, opal, pearl, rose quartz

Finances, stabilizing: jet, ruby, green goldstone, green calcite, green tourmaline

Finding lost objects, people: peridot, snakeskin agate, golden topaz, green moss agate (lost treasure or money)

Fluid retention: aquamarine, moonstone, river rock

Focus: apatite, fluorite, Herkimer diamond, pearl, quartz crystal

Fortune, good: bloodstone, lodestone (magnetite), moonstone, tree agate

Friendship: aventurine, green moss agate, apatite

G

Gallbladder (protect): carnelian, chrysoberyl, angelite

Gambling luck: aventurine, moonstone, fiery opal

Gardening & agriculture: Herkimer diamond, jasper, lepidolite

Generosity: citrine, dolomite, jasper

Grace: blue lace agate, rhodonite, zincite

Grief: amethyst, apache tear, aqua aura, bloodstone, Botswana agate, chrysocolla, carnelian, citrine, chrysoprase, galena, jasper, jet, lapis lazuli, onyx, pyrite, rose quartz, smoky quartz, watermelon tourmaline

Grounding: agate, apache tears, bloodstone, Boji stones (Kansas pop rocks), brecciated jasper, candle quartz, carnelian, Cuprite, dalmatian jasper, fluorite, hematite, obsidian, salt, smoky quartz, sulphur, tiger iron (mugglestone), topaz, unakite

Growth: blue lace agate, quartz crystal, smoky quartz, tigers eye

Guilt: copper, rose quartz, ruby, sodalite

H

Hair loss: aragonite, chalcopyrite, franklinite, galena

Happiness: amethyst, amazonite, apophyllite, aventurine, blue lace agate, blue quartz, bornite (peacock ore), carnelian, chrysoprase, euclase, gold, Herkimer diamond, moonstone, pyrite, rainbow crystals, rose quartz, smoky quartz

Harmonious environment: amber, amethyst, green millenium™, petrified wood, rose quartz, tigers eye

Harmony: agate, amethyst, apatite, carnelian, chiastolite, clear quartz, emerald, jade, peridot, rhodochrosite, rhodonite, selenite, multi-colored tourmaline, tree agate

Headache, general: amber, amethyst, angelite, aquamarine, black jade, bloodstone, blue agate, blue aventurine, blue lace agate, optical calcite, cavansite, celestite, charoite, cherry opal, chrysacolla, common opal, diamond, dioptase, emerald, fire agate, green aventurine, green tourmaline, blue chalcedony, iolite, jade, jet, lapis lazuli, malachite, moss agate, blue obsidian, pearl, phenacite (phenakite), purple fluorite, rhodochrosite, rose quartz, silicon, sodalite, sugilite, sulphur, stilbite, tiger eye, turquoise. *See migraine headache and tension headache.*

Healing and health (general): agate, amber, amethyst, amazonite, aventurine, azurite, celestite, calcite, citrine, charoite, chlorite, chrysacolla, chrysoprase, coral, danburite, epidote, fuschite, garnet, green calcite, green moss agate, green tourmaline, infinite, jet, labradorite, lepidolite, moonstone, peridot, petrified wood, phantom quartz, pink tourmaline, quartz crystals, jasper, malachite, rhodochrosite, rutilated quartz, self-healed quartz, smoky quartz, watermelon tourmaline

Heart (physical): amazonite, amber, beryl, garnet, gaspeite, hematite, lapis lazuli, green obsidian, onyx, peach aventurine, rhodonite, ruby

Honesty: amazonite, celestite, chrysocolla, citrine, emerald, purple fluorite, jet, kyanite, lapis lazuli, pearl, ruby, selenite, sodalite, tiger's eye

Honor: gold, jet, euclase, labradorite

Hostility (removing): chlorite, abalone, howlite

Housekeeping: ammonite, mother of pearl, limonite

Humility: jade, agate, angelite, celestite, moldavite

I

Imagination: aventurine, yellow calcite, green fluorite

Immune system: amethyst, citrine, epidote, pearl, snow quartz, sulphur, topaz, obsidian, picture jasper, rhodochrosite, rhodonite

Implant removal – psychic: ajoite, apache tears, chlorite, petrified wood, purple fluorite

Incest recovery: thulite, celestite, rose quartz, aventurine

Incontinence: petrified wood, charoite, feldspar

Individuality (strength to stress): carnelian, blue topaz, lepidolite

Infection (abscess): pearl, pyrite, quartz

Inferiority (feelings of): chrysoprase, garnet, lapis lazuli

Infertility (physical): carnelian, garnet, quartz scepter, rose quartz, shiva lingam

Inflammation: pyrite, turquoise, calcite, holey stone

Inhibitions: opal, tourmaline, red jasper

Inner awareness: apache tears, rose quartz, shattuckite, Boji™ stones,

Inner child: amber, cobaltocalcite, imperial topaz, morganite, rainbow Boji stone (Kansas pop rocks), rainbow quartz, quartz crystal with another crystal inside

Inner growth: rhodonite, falcon's eye, mugglestone

Inner peace: amethyst, apatite, aquamarine, aventurine, blue topaz, blue tourmaline, calcite, celestite, chrysocolla, blue fluorite, falcon's eye (blue tigers eye), Herkimer diamond, jade, jasper, kunzite, lepidolite, malachite, opal, rose quartz, selenite, sugilite

Insect bites: moonstone, green fluorite, petrified wood, fulgarite

Insomnia: amethyst, celestite, emerald, hematite, labradorite, lapis, lepidolite, smoky quartz, sodalite, tiger iron, zircon

Intellect: aquamarine, agate, amazonite, ametrine, apatite, aquamarine, aventurine, azurite, bloodstone, celestite, chalcedony, coral, diopside, emerald, galena, honey calcite, malachite, obsidian, pyrite, rose quartz, sodalite, tektite, topaz, turquoise

Intestinal / digestive: amber, aquamarine, barite, celestine, chrysocolla, citrine, clear quartz, cuprite, pyrite, jasper, labradorite, moss agate, obsidian, onyx, peridot, smoky quartz, thulite

Irritable bowel syndrome: orange calcite, orange millenium™

Intuitive awareness: amazonite, amethyst, azurite, chrysolite, emerald, euclase, lapis, onyx, sodalite, yellow calcite

J

Jealousy (dispels): eudialyte, peridot, malachite, lepidolite, rhodochrosite

Joy: emerald, pearl, diamond

K

Kidney / bladder: anhydrite (angelite), amber, bloodstone, green calcite, carnelian, chrysoberyl, coral, Cuprite, jade, jasper, orange calcite, rhodochrosite, smoky quartz

Kindness: azurite, celestite, chalcedony, chrysoberyl, chrysocolla, jasper, kunzite, morganite, rhodochrosite, rhodonite, rose quartz, pink tourmaline, turquoise

Kundalini: garnet, jet, red jasper, lava stone

L

Laughter: crazy lace agate, petrified wood, rainbow calcite

Law enforcement: fuchsite, cinnabar, aragonite

Leadership/management: fossils, trilobite, amber

Legal issues: amethyst, bloodstone, hematite, lodestone (magnetite)

Life purpose (discover): desert rose, celestite, moldavite

Liver: carnelian, jasper, fluorite, apache tears

Logic: sodalite, kunzite, hiddenite, galena

Loneliness: dolomite, aquamarine, malachite

Longevity: diamond, fossils, jasper, tree agate

Love: amber, coral, emerald, hiddenite, kunzite, jade, laramar stone, pink calcite, pink tourmaline, rose quartz, rhodocrosite, ruby, selenite,

Loyalty: dalmatian jasper, moonstone, danburite

Luck: agate, aquamarine, aventurine, copper, jade, malachite, obsidian, pyrite, snow quartz, smoky quartz, tigers eye, tiger iron (mugglestone

Lungs: peach aventurine, holey stone, pyrite, rutilated quartz, galena, peridot

M

Manifestation: carnelian, emerald, green calcite, citrine, dolomite, labradorite, lapis, moldavite, obsidian, opal, quartz crystals, topaz

Marriage: pearl, peridot, diamond, tanzanite, ruby

Master Healer Stones: amethyst, rose quartz, rhodizite, elestial crystal, malachite, selenite, sugilite, Tibetan quartz,

Mastery: onyx, Apache tears, sardonyx

Mathematics/analytical pursuits: angelite, diopside, hematite, sodalite

Meditation: amethyst, ametrine, aqua aura, aquamarine, azurite, celestite, chrysoprase, clear quartz, chrysocolla, dumortierite (blue quartz), fluorite, iolite, kunzite, kyanite, labradorite, lapis, prehnite, sea shells, selenite, snow quartz, sugilite, topaz, yellow calcite

Melancholy: dioptase, agate, cymophane

Memory: blue calcite, carnelian, emerald, honey calcite, onyx, pyrite, quartz crystals, rhodochrosite

Menopause: moonstone, cinnabar, red calcite

Mental clarity: amber, aquamarine, aventurine, blue quartz, citrine, clear quartz, Herkimer diamond, sodalite, tiger eye, topaz

Merchants stone: citrine, fuschite, ruby, quartz

Metamorphosis: black obsidian, tourmaline, tourmalinated quartz

Migraine headache: jet (natural), phenacite (phenakite), purple fluorite, rose quartz

Miracles: blue lace agate, celestite, azeztulite

Money (attracts): green tourmaline, aventurine, jade

Mood swings: citrine, diamond, variscite

Morality (improves): gold, angelite, green kyanite

Muscle strength: abalone, amazonite, apatite, chrysocolla, emerald

Muscular cramping: cuprite, azurite, wulfenite, prehnite

N

Nail problems: apatite, tiger iron, quartz crystal, silica

Narrow mindedness: epidote, yellow calcite, petrified wood

Negative energy (dispel, transmute): black tourmaline, black obsidian, quartz, Boji™ stone, blue kyanite

Negativity: ajoite, carnelian, citrine, jade, blue kyanite, malachite, obsidian, rutilated quartz, selenite

Nervous system: alexandrite, amazonite, aquamarine, apatite, Botswana agate, fire agate, emerald, galena, lapis lazuli, morganite, peridot, sugilite, tourmaline

Neuralgia (nerve pain): chrysoprase, blue celestite, Herkimer diamond

New beginnings: chrysoprase, moonstone, apophyllite

Nightmares / night terrors: citrine, dalmatian jasper, dioptase, atlantisite, flint, red sandstone, holey stone

Nurturing: jasper, amethyst, rose quartz, lepidolite

O

Obsessive/Compulsive Disorder: eudialyte, lepidocrosite, ametrine

Old hurts: rhodonite, moqui marble, petrified wood, peacock ore (bornite)

Order out of chaos: fluorite, hematite, lepidolite

Organization: bloodstone, brecciated jasper, dumortierite (blue quartz), fluorite, lapis lazuli, lepidolite, mugglestone, red jasper

Osteoporosis: amazonite, howlite, calcite

P

Pain relief: amber, amethyst, dolomite, green calcite, hematite, howlite, lapis, lodestone, mugglestone. (tiger iron)

Pancreas: carnelian, moonstone, tigers eye

Panic attacks: epidote, lepidolite, driftwood

Paralysis: petrified wood, moonstone, howlite

Parkinson's disease: cuprite, opal, clear quartz crystal, moldavite

Passion: emerald, garnet, ruby

Past life: ajoite, amber, amethyst, aquamarine, carnelian, holey stones, obsidian, phantom crystals, petrified wood

Patience: amber, amethyst, azurite, chrysoprase,

Peace: amethyst, apatite, aquamarine, blue quartz, chevron amethyst, chrysocolla, fluorite, lepidolite, malachite, rose quartz, sugilite

Perception: danburite, epidote, black tourmaline

Phobias: aquamarine, chrysoprase, clear quartz

Physical energy: calcite, carnelian, Herkimer diamond, quartz, tigers eye

Physical strength: bloodstone, garnet, Herkimer diamond, quartz

Physical trauma: bloodstone, kyanite (especially black kyanite), seraphenite

Pilot's stone (air): malachite, moonstone, azeztulite

Pilot's stone (water): larimar, dioptase, aquamarine, blue calcite, holey stone

Pineal Gland: moldovite, tektite, Ajoite, calcite

Pituitary gland: moonstone, rhodonite, selenite

Plant growth: Boji™ stones (Kansas pop rocks), brecciated jasper, quartz, malachite

Pleasure: citrine, red jasper, charoite

PMS (Pre-Menstrual Syndrome): dolomite, lapis, rose quartz, unakite

Positive attitude: aventurine, hematite, obsidian, zoisite

Post surgical: bloodstone, coal, jet

Power: aquamarine, charoite, epidote (personal), red jasper, rutilated quartz, quartz, tiger eye

Prophesy: prehnite, moqui marble, Boji™ stone, bornite

Prosperity / abundance / money: aventurine, amethyst, aqua aura, bloodstone, calcite, citrine, green moss agate, Herkimer diamond, jade, jasper, malachite, peridot, salt, tiger's eye, turquoise

Protection from negativity: black obsidian, black tourmaline, kunzite, quartz, blue kyanite,

Protection (children): agate, jasper, solar goddess aura crystal

Protection (from evil): agate, black tourmaline, Herkimer diamond, holey stone, malachite, pyrite, quartz, salt, snowflake obsidian, turquoise

Protection (general): agate, amber, apache tears, aventurine, calcite, carnelian, citrine, black tourmaline, chiastolite, fire agate, fluorite, fossils, Herkimer diamond, honey calcite, howlite, jade, jasper, jet, labradorite, lapis, lepidolite, malachite, moonstone, pyrite, quartz, ruby, rutilated quartz, salt, sardonyx, shark teeth, snowflake obsidian, tigers eye, tourmaline, tree agate, turquoise

Psychic abilities/intuition: amazonite, amethyst, apatite, azeztulite, azurite, Botswana agate, cavansite, celestite, covelite, emerald, fire agate, fluorite, garnet, green calcite, Herkimer diamonds, holey stone, moqui marbles, kyanite, labradorite, lapis, meteorites, moonstone, opal, orange calcite, quartz, rhodizite, selenite, super seven, tektite, turquoise

Psychic shield / protection: ajoite, amethyst, Boji™ stones (Kansas pop rocks), fluorite, blue kyanite, pyrite, ruby, moqui marbles, red calcite, howlite, steatite.

PTSD (post traumatic stress disorder): hematite, richterite, hiddenite

Public speaking: celestite, azurite, blue lace agate

Purification: calcite, fluorite, chrysocolla, halite, salt

R

Radiation exposure: black tourmaline, amethyst, azeztulite

Reconciliation: calcite, Herkimer diamond, kunzite, rose quartz, rhodocrosite

Relationships: bixbite, dalmatian jasper (long term), diamond (esp. long term), fluorite, ruby

Relaxation: bronzite, chevron amethyst, dalmatian jasper, jasper, red jasper, richterite

Releasing blockages: ametrine, bloodstone, fluorite, malachite, obsidian

Reliability: hematite, lapis lazuli, sugalite

Relieving burdens: lodestone. coral, pearl

Removing obstacles: kunzite, clear quartz, ruby

Repressed issues: Botswana agate, epidote, unakite

Reproductive system: orange calcite, red calcite, garnet, ruby

Responsibility: leopardskin jasper, smoky quartz, topaz

Romance: garnet, amber, diamonds, emerald, pyrope garnets, red coral, red garnet, red tourmaline, rose quartz, ruby, sardonyx

S

Schizophrenia: celestial quartz, kunzite, larimar, lepidolite

Scrying: obsidian, quartz, amethyst

Self-awareness/self-discovery: chevron amethyst, ametrine, sunstone

Self-confidence: agate, aragonite, citrine, dolomite, garnet, labradorite, malachite, moss agate, rhodonite, ruby, sodalite, tigers eye, tiger iron, tourmaline, turquoise

Self-discipline: dumortierite (blue quartz), kunzite, tiger iron

Self-empowerment: erythrite, diamond, rose quartz, rhodizite

Self-esteem: amazonite, carnelian, copper, kunzite, rhodochrosite, green moss agate

Self-expression: chryosphase, howlite, rhodochrosite

Self-love: aquamarine, danburite, feldspar, kunzite, labradorite, lepidolite, rhodochrosite, rhodonite, rose quartz, ruby, sodalite

Self-realization: aventurine, sunstone, malachite

Selfishness: howlite, lepidolite, obsidian

Sensuality/sexuality: amber, Botswana agate, carnelian, citrine, garnet, jade, mexican fire opal, red calcite, ruby, rutilated quartz, onyx

Serenity: aquamarine, blue quartz (dumortierite), blue tourmaline, celestite, chrysocolla, emerald, falcon's eye (blue tigers eye), jade, jasper, kunzite, kyanite, smoky quartz, turquoise,

Shamanic work: iolite, moqui marbles/moki balls, obsidian, holey stones, yellow calcite, bornite, peacock ore, Boji™ Stones

Shielding: amber, apache tears, black tourmaline, Boji™ stones, hematite, labradorite, peridot, smoky quartz

Sinusitis: lapis, rhodochrosite, smithsonite, blue calcite

Skin / skin disorders: apophyllite, amethyst, aventurine, azurite / malachite, Botswana agate, carnelian, chrysotile, corundum (sapphire, ruby), crazy lace agate, dumortierite, fancy jasper, garnet (skin protection), green jasper, moonstone, moss agate, epidote, mother of pearl, picture jasper, rainforest jasper (rhyolite), spinel, turquoise

Sleep disorders: amethyst, aventurine, hematite, peridot, moonstone

Smoking – quit: Botswana agate, petrified wood, Herkimer diamonds

Sorrow: apache tears, dolomite, celestite,

Soul movement / travel – above astral: blue calcite, apatite, iolite, larimar stone

Spirit contact: azeztulite, jade, herderite, prehnite, moonstone, red sandstone, holey stones, celestite, selenite, quartz

Spiritual development: amethyst, celestite, citrine, epidote, gaspeite, quartz, selenite, topaz, peacock ore

Spirituality: amethyst, apache tears, calcite, citrine, clear quartz, hematite, Herkimer diamond, iolite, lepidolite, meteorites (tektite), pearl, rhodocrosite, selnite, topaz, sugilite, turquoise

Spleen: fluorite, hematite, lapis, tigers eye

Stability: celestite, chrysoprase, citrine, hematite, obsidian, petrified wood, smoky quartz, tiger iron (mugglestone)

Stamina: chalcedony, crazy lace agate, dolomite, sodalite, tiger iron

Stomach problems: Botswana agate, citrine, peridot, jasper, obsidian, citrine, ametrine

Strength: agate, carnelian, citrine, granite, hematite, Herkimer diamonds, richterite, tigers eye, tiger iron (mugglestone), rutilated quartz

Stress: aragonite, azurite-malachite, bloodstone, brecciated jasper, calcite, chevron amethyst, dioptase, dolomite, fluorite, gold, hematite, howlite, kunzite, labradorite, lepidolite, moonstone, peridot, picasso marble, richterite, rose quartz, smoky quartz, staurolite, sunstone, turquoise

Success (personal): aventurine, aqua aura, citrine, green moss agate, green tourmaline

Success (business/career): aventurine, bloodstone, citrine, chrysoprase, lepidolite, leopard skin jasper, malachite, petrified wood

T

Teaching: geode, lapis, kyanite, sodalite

Teamwork: smoky quartz, quartz crystal cluster, bornite

Teeth/gums: agate, amazonite, aquamarine, calcite, dolomite, fluorite, howlite, malachite

Tension headache: amethyst, blue lace agate, cat's eye, chrysacolla, lapis lazuli, tanzanite

Thinking process: dolomite, fluorite, hematite

Throat: amber, ammonite, angelite, beryl, blue calcite, blue topaz, chalcopyrite, chrysocolla, galena, larimar, malachite, morganite, opal, tigers eye

Thyroid: blue calcite, rhodonite, amber, super seven stone

Tissue regeneration: carnelian, citrine, flint, malachite, turquoise

Toxins: amber, amethyst, Botswana agate, citrine, leopard skin jasper, tree agate, rutilated quartz

Tranquility: blue lace agate, larimar stone, jasper

Transformation: bronzite, charoite, lepidolite, malachite, obsidian, moqui marbles

Travel by water: aquamarine, dumortierite, clear quartz

Travel: amethyst, aquamarine, chalcedony, Herkimer diamond, jet, malachite, tigers eye

Truth: amazonite, apophyllite, celestite, citrine, emerald, fluorite, kyanite, lapis lazuli, selenite, sodalite, tiger's eye

U

Ulcers: agate, chrysocolla , peridot, rose quartz

Unconditional love: kunzite, rhodocrosite, rhodonite, rose quartz

V

Vertigo: cuprite, chrysacolla, malachite, sapphire, Herkimer diamond, rose quartz, variscite

Victimization: black tourmaline, charoite, chrysoprase, garnet, green calcite, hematite, jade, leopard skin jasper, malachite, orange millennium™, rose quartz, rutilated quartz, self-healed quartz crystals, thulite

Vigor / virility: tiger iron (mugglestone), hematite, charoite

Visualization: iolite, green tourmaline, moqui marbles

Vitality: chalcedony,

W

Warrior Stone: obsidian, tiger iron,

Water (fear of): aquamarine, azurite, blue quartz, chalcedony, kyanite, sapphire

Weight loss: blue Peruvian opal, citrine, green tourmaline, moonstone, picasso marble (jasper), rose quartz, sulphur, unakite (ideal weight)

Weight gain: citrine, unakite (ideal weight)

Will power: alexandrite, blue tigers eye (hawk's eye), garnet, hematite, red jasper, sapphire, tigers eye, tiger iron (mugglestone)

Wisdom: amber, calcite, clear quartz, fulgarite, jade, labradorite, lapis, malachite, moonstone, petrified wood, smoky quartz, snowflake obsidian, sodalite, tree agate

Wishes: moonstone, smoky quartz, unakite

Worries: green jade, petrified wood, rhodochrosite, tourmaline

Wrinkles: azurite, lepidolite, rose quartz, gem silica

Y

Yellow Fever – yellow calcite, topaz, smoky quartz

Yellow Jaundice – selenite, limonite, pink calcite, bloodstone, red jasper

Yeast Infection (mouth): chalcopyrite (peacock ore), kyanite, lapis lazuli, quartz, sodalite

Yeast Infection (systemic): amber, aventurine, chalcopyrite (peacock ore), citrine, garnet, quartz, sodalite, yellow jasper

Yin/Yang – lodestone, Ametrine, howlite

HOW TO FORM A RELATIONSHIP
WITH CRYSTALS AND STONES

It is important to know that every rock, stone, crystal, seashell, petrified wood, mineral, etc. contains the essence of consciousness within it. To contact this essence, this energy, all we need do is .... Breathe.

Our breath is powerful. Crystals and stones don't care about coffee or garlic breath; all they can feel is the purity of our intent when we hold them up before our mouths and greet them. This is how I form a relationship with my rocks, stones and crystals. I greet them by raising them to my lips and speaking to them. I might say something along the lines of ... "Hello crystal, you are beautiful and I am so very happy to meet you. I enjoy your positive energy and admire your beauty. I invite you into my life, look forward to being friends and enjoying a long relationship with you."

I also ask my stones if they would like to go here or there with me. Before I leave the house, I will ask my crystals .. "I'm going to town, who would like to go with me?" Usually, I will 'feel' which of my stones wants to go, which may feel they will be needed by those I meet, or those whom I will touch in some way. One day I asked my crystals who would like to go with me, and my Christ Commune Crystal and Tibetan Double Terminated crystal wanted to go with me. I placed one in each pocket of my jeans and left the house. Didn't think about it until I was at a counter paying for a drink and the Christ Commune Crystal prompted me to show it to the cashier. As I showed the young man the crystal, I could see his demeanor change from being nervous about his first day, to feeling more at peace with his surroundings. Things like this happen to me a lot and once you become more at ease with your crystals and stones, you, too will hear what your stones have to say to you, too.

Your stones might want to take a shower with you, or go swimming with you, or travel with you. I always travel with a collection of stones, some I give away, leave here and there, and others just come for the experience.

I work with crystals all day long during consultations with people and sometimes I am prompted to send the working crystal to them … which I do. I am so happy to share crystal wisdom with every one I meet. The crystals and stones tell me who they would like to be sent to, and where they would like to travel. I have gifted the Gulf of Mexico with numerous crystals for healing and clearing. Where they go is not my business; I just know that when they say … 'take me here' and I do .. everything feels right. If by chance, I don't listen for one reason or another, it seems to be just fine … my crystal friends know and trust that they will be heard for the next outing. They are very forgiving beings. The operative word here is "BE-ings" because … inside every rock, crystal, stone, sea shell, piece of petrified wood, driftwood, hunk of copper, gold, silver, platinum --- is a BE-ing just waiting for us to communicate.

Crystals are a gift from the Universe to us to be used for the good of the whole and for achieving our highest purpose. Crystals and stones are natural beings that readily accept our friendship. Use of crystals and stones must first come from the heart fueled by pure intent. No matter how you come by your crystal or stone, whether it is a gift, a purchase, or a find, it is important to establish a relationship first and foremost. Admire your crystal and stone for its beauty, but appreciate it for its integrity and ability to balance and transmit harmony, joy and fulfillment. Be the crystal!

The first draw to a stone for me is its energy, which I feel through the way it looks. It may be the color, or the shape, or simply just a compelling pull to touch it or move it. Some rocks and stones may not necessarily want to come with me, but may ask to be moved. Some other rocks speak to me through their beauty.

Appreciating a rock's, stone's or crystal's beauty is the initial way I make friends with it. I hold it, look at it with love, try to get a feel for its experience initially, and then gradually give it the time and space to communicate with me. I still have my very first quartz crystal that I 'met' in a metaphysical shop in Reisterstown, Maryland some 25 years ago, and have kept rocks and stones that I met in my travels over the years going back some 45 years or more. Why? Because we have become friends who have traveled this life together and that is a very strong bond indeed.

When looking for a rock, crystal or stone, be sure to choose your own. Don't give away your power by having someone else choose a stone for you. Go to a rock shop, feel them, touch them, ask them if they would like to be with you. That is how I chose my first crystal. I looked in the basket of crystals on the shelf, handled them, felt them, and then … touched them to my brow chakra. This helped me to know which stone was for me because I could feel its energy clearly and see it with my Tisra T'il. If you are gifting a stone for someone else, ask the stone if they would like to meet that person. Envision the person and then touch the stone to your brow chakra … the crystal will tell you whether it wants to be a part of that person's life or not.

Don't worry about stones that have been dyed, heated, sanded, cut or otherwise manipulated in some way. Each stone still carries its original energy. For instance, clear crystal is sometimes exposed to heated vapors of gold, silver and platinum that cause the crystal to change color. Because of this process, we have Aqua Aura, Angel Aura and Opal Aura crystals that are powerful in their own right. And remember, dyed stones still have the energy of love that you place in it.

If you've lost a crystal or stone and terribly miss that stone, think of it this way -- All the love and positive energy you placed into that rock or crystal is now being used to soothe someone else, now healing another who needed it more than you did. Stones have a way of letting us know that it is time for them to move on. We need to honor that code and trust the process that good will come from our loss by it being another's gain for good purpose.

Once you share love and energy with an object, no matter what it is … that love never fades. The energy continues to pulse out into the Universe where it will make its way to the place that it needs to be.

Right now, as I write, I have rocks and stones on the floor of my truck that have been traveling with me since my trip out west in April 2010; and I have a pelican feather on my dashboard that keeps me company when I drive! Living things given to us to love, respect and use for our own betterment – treasured trinkets from the Creator !

HOW TO CLEAR AND PROGRAM CRYSTALS AND STONES

Crystals and stones are receivers, transmitters and storage containers that hold energy. Scientific proof of this statement is the fact that crystals have been used to transmit radio waves between a sender unit and receiver unit. You utilize crystal technology every time you turn on your television, radio or computer. Crystals and stones also hold thought forms. When this is done consciously, it is called "programming."

The term "Programming" is used because this process is similar to computer programming. Information or commands are stored in the molecular structure of the quartz crystal as magnetic charged data. Thoughts are energy, and they are magnetic in form. All data in programmed crystals are stored as thought forms. Thought forms are pictures and/or other sensory data, powered or intensified by emotion. The Brow Chakra (between both the eyes) method is an effective way of programming a crystal.

Remember to first ask your crystal what is its original programming and if it wants to change or not. If a crystal finds its way into your hands, it is entirely possible that it has come to you with its own program intended to heal and help you in its present state. Ask .. then listen for an answer. Sometimes, it helps to place your crystal in water first. Water is a perfect conductor of electricity and makes it easier for you to hear their magic song.

The Brow Chakra Method

First, and importantly, determine the purpose of the program. Next, and also importantly, think of the end result you would have if the program worked. Place the crystal against your brow. The direction the crystal is pointing does not matter; what matters is that you think positive thoughts and envision your desire while you hold the crystal to your forehead.

Close your eyes and envision yourself entering your crystal.

Next, picture the desired end result happening inside your crystal. Create it with as many of your senses as you can. See it, smell it, touch it, hear it, taste it, make it real. When it feels real; come out of your crystal and open your eyes.

What you have just done is programmed your crystal for your intention.

The Breath Method

The Breath Method of programming a crystal or stone is also effective. As with the Brow Chakra Method, it is important to think of the end result, create it in your mind. Bring your crystal up to your mouth. As you envision your desired result, breathe exactly what you see and desire into your crystal by speaking the words directly into it.

If you are going to program your crystal for abundance and prosperity, speak words similar to these into your crystal: *"Crystal, I program you to attract abundance and prosperity to my atmosphere My intent is pure and I program you to attract to me what will serve my highest good."*

If you are going to program your crystal for success in an endeavor, speak words similar to these into your crystal: *"Crystal, I program you to direct me toward success in (named endeavor, taking class, changing career, etc.). My intent is pure and I program you to promote my desired result as it serves my highest good."*

Remember, do not program your crystal or stone to impact another's free will one way or the other, because there are karmic implications once you engage another into your desired result.

How To Clear Your Crystal:

To clear a crystal, hold it in your hand, bring the crystal up to your mouth and repeat the Light Invocation three times while breathing into the crystal.

" I speak to the Light of the Creator within. I declare myself to be a clear and perfect channel. Light is my guide."

Another invocation to use to clear a crystal is borrowed from Native history ~~ and involves allowing the crystal to maintain its integrity and gifts while clearing it from negativity:

"May the essence of this crystal remain true to itself. May any energies that are disharmonious and otherwise negative be removed and cleared. I invoke the energies of clarity, brilliance and light to permeate the atmosphere of this crystal NOW."

Every ailment carries within it negative emotions. Do you know many people who are ill and are happy about it? Probably not. When balancing occurs, the negative emotions are purged from the body and often become embedded in the client's crystals. Repeating the Light Invocation three times can neutralize all negative emotions in an object.

You may also utilize the energies of the four elements to clear your crystal – Fire, Water, Air and Earth.

You may bury your crystal in soil for 24 hours with the intent of grounding and clearing it. Or, you may set your crystal on top of the soil in the light of the sun and the moon for three days.

Becky Young of Sweet Surrender Crystal Mines shared with me to keep 'mine mud' to clear and cleanse crystals because the mud in which the crystals grow is like 'birthing water' to a crystal. It re-energizes, recalibrates and refreshes the crystal, like going back to its Mother, and … indeed it is!

Blowing your breath over a crystal can also clear it of negative energies.

Use Fire by smudging your crystals with sage or incense.

You may also invoke the energies of the Universal Life Force using Usui Reiki or Celtic Reiki to cleanse and clear your crystal and stones.

Perhaps too easy to consider, you may also just ask the Universe to clear and cleanse your crystal with pure intent and love.

These suggestions are important whether you are a professional or a concerned individual who simply wants to help others. When you become more experienced, you will use crystals for many purposes.

NOTE: Keep in mind that some crystals may not 'want' to be cleared because they have their own gifts to offer us. Before you clear your crystal, please … respect its essence and ask it if it has anything to share, and if it wishes to be cleared.

For example, clusters, which are multiple crystals together in one piece, are excellent for creating a change in your immediate environment.

You can use sets of crystals to create powerful grid fields to charge water, food, clothing, and to change the energy field of an entire room.

Keep a crystal in your car or vehicle and program it for protection from the errors of other drivers and also to protect you from making critical mistakes while behind the wheel. You may also program a crystal to protect your vehicle from being entered with mal-intent by others who may consider you a victim.

The variety of uses for crystals can expand in direct proportion to your knowledge and your intent.

However, using crystals and stones is only suggested for positivity and pure intentions in service to the All That Is as the needs of the good of the whole are impacted.

How To Clean Your Crystals

Clearing is the process of changing negative emotions to positive emotions. Anyone who holds a crystal and is having bad feelings or experiencing negative emotions, may imprint those emotions into the crystal. The most effective method for clearing a crystal is to hold or touch it with your hand. Repeat the following light invocation three times.

The light invocation is as follows;

" I join with the Light of the Creator within and declare myself to be a clear and perfect channel. Light is my guide."

By the time you have completed the third repetition; the negative emotion will be gone.

The Light Invocation clears out any negative energy that the crystal or stone may have absorbed. And, by using the Light Invocation, you also increase the overall energy field around you in your personal atmosphere.

Cleansing is a process of reducing the negative emotional energy level to the crystal to the point where the emotional energy can no longer affect you. There are a number of ways you can cleanse your stones. Bury the crystal in either dry salt or submerge it in a saline solution of ½ cup sea salt to one gallon of water for at least one day.

Other ways of cleansing a crystal or stone is to allow it to sit in the light of the moon overnight. By the same token, you may also allow your crystals or stones to sit in the bright sunshine during the day.

You may bathe with your crystal or stones. If you are fond of showers, take your crystals and stones with you to the shower and form a grid around the inside of the enclosure. If you are fond of baths, you can do the same thing, form a grid around the outside of the tub with your crystals and then one by one, wash them in the water with you. This forms a bond with your crystals and stones, as well as cleanses them.

How To Bond With Your Crystals

Speaking of bonding with your crystals and stones ~~ it is good to carry a crystal or stone with you all the time, in your pocket, your purse, your handbag, belt-pack or back-pack. Ladies, you can place your crystal or stone in your bra close to your heart, as I do many times. You can change the stone or crystal that you carry so that you form a relationship with all of your stones. The importance is that you recognize and honor the light of the Creator Source within each stone and crystal by acknowledging its presence. Tell your crystal and/or stone that you enjoy its company and invite its participation in all that you do.

Let your crystal know your intent is to form a bond, a relationship with it, one that will last a lifetime, or until you both no longer require the bond. Sometimes, we may feel the need to infuse the crystal with our energies and then pass it along to another for their use and healing. Allow your spirit to guide you and listen to the small voice within when it comes to befriending your stones and crystals.

How To Ground Yourself to A Crystal or Stone

Grounding yourself to a crystal or stone helps you to re-establish your connection to Lady Gaia, our Mother Earth. Not enough energy input from Mother Earth leaves us fatigued, tired and restless. Too much energy input, whether it is environmental or emotional, can cause your energies to scatter, separating you from your body. You may feel disoriented, confused and generally out of touch with yourself. Your crystals and stones act as a grounding force, tuning you in to the natural energies of the Earth. Here are two effective visualization techniques that help you to ground yourself with your crystal or stone.

Technique No.1: Preferably, perform this technique outside amongst the plants and trees. If that is not possible, use the power of visualization to create your own sacred space.

Place your crystal in your pockets or better, tape them to your body. You can place them inside your bra or tight fitting undergarment so that the stone is against your skin. Stand in an area large enough to extend your arms out from your side without touching anything. With your arms by your side, take a deep breath and raise your arms into a horizontal position at the shoulder, palms down. As you breathe in, imagine you are drawing in the earth energies through you palms, feel a tingling sensation. Hold your arm position and your breath for a moment and then release your breath with a forceful "hahhh," while pushing your palms down towards the ground, imagine you are firing your energy into the earth. You may need to do this two or three times until you notice subtly how much more you feel connected to yourself and to the earth.

Technique No.2: This technique involves a meditative visualization and can be performed either outdoors in your yard or indoors in your favorite spot where you will not be distracted. Get comfortable, sitting or lying down. Place your crystals or stones in a grid around you, or if you only have one crystal or stone, place it close to your heart. Imagine that you are a tree, a stately redwood, a majestic oak, a graceful Japanese Maple, or any other tree with which you feel a kinship.

Visualize your roots growing down through your feet to the center of the earth. Feel your roots attach to the Earth deep within the soil and then, begin to draw the Earth energy up through your roots, your feet, ankles, calves, thighs, to your root chakra energy center. Feel the powerful energy tingle through your hips, sacral energy center, and lower body, your solar plexus energy center and middle torso, up through your heart energy center and chest.

Feel your hands begin to tingle with the flow of this natural energy, up your arms, shoulders, your throat energy center and neck, face, and up through your crown chakra energy center at the top of your head bursting through with a rushing sound as a rainbow spray of light and color.

Hear the wind rush through your leaves and limbs as the rainbow array of color flows down your body and is drawn back up through the bottom of your feet in a continuous cycle, in three cyclic pulses.

When you are done, release the grasp of your roots and slowly open your eyes, returning to your quiet place. Before you get up, take time to relish the grounding refreshment of the pulsing energies. Go about your day now, totally and completely grounded to Earth and Earth's energies through your crystal.

How To Heal With a Crystal

It has been explained that a physician treats the physical body, the psychologist treats the mind and the clergy treats the soul. However, it is the metaphysician who works to balance all three – body, mind and spirit.

The way that life progresses, we soon discover that if we learn to balance the energies of all our parts – body, mind and spirit, we then open the door to greater health, harmony, joy and fulfillment. We recognize the signs and understand the methods ~ that there is more here than simply meets the eye!

The key to all healing is through our use of the Universal Life Force Energy ~~ or simply, energy. Energy is in everything – from the tiniest grain of sand to the largest mountain. Anything that blocks or hinders the movement of energy weakens our personal atmosphere. When a single cell is weakened by energy deprivation, it sends out a signal to the brain asking for more energy to alleviate the problem and keep itself in balance. And so, we, as human beings, do the same thing.

There are conditions that make it difficult for the brain to function normally, such as medications, recreational drugs, alcohol and stress. These influences cause an 'altered' state where signals can get crossed or at worst, not be received at all.

When the brain is in a state of energy abundance, it hears the message loudly and clearly. The appropriate amount of energy is then sent out to the needy cell that causes it to operate as expected, rejuvenating, replacing and maintaining balance. Once the correct amount of energy is restored, the system that signals the need is turned off and the system returns to normal.

Crystals and stones supply energy; that is one of their various jobs here on Mother Earth. They have no ill or side effects. They give the cells the necessary energy, which is vital for repairing and maintaining health of an individual.

When the mind is linked to crystals and stones, they serve as an amplifier to increase the healing process and transmission of positive energy. Crystal energy can be used to pre-charge an area before surgery to reduce the trauma to the cells, and it can be used after surgery to replace the energy loss caused by that trauma. Crystals also increase the output of Reiki energies during healing sessions and are often used by Reiki practitioners. Metaphysicians use crystals and stones to bless, heal and lock in a positivity treatment.

Drugs and surgery operate through the physical body. Crystals and stones amplify and access all levels of mind, emotion, spirit, and body. The thoughts and emotions human beings generate or absorb from others create their physical condition. For healing to last, all levels need to balance and stabilize.

Crystal and stone healing is only concerned with energy. The physical body is the end result of energy. If the energies of the body can be stimulated and balanced, then the physical body must repair itself, as an end result, as well. This is the Law of Nature – cause and effect that filters down through all the dimensions.

Crystal Healing is non-intrusive and non-invasive. It only adjusts energy fields. The results are fast and gentle. Used together with science and medicine, crystals can accelerate healing and reach areas difficult to work with by conventional methods. As we enter the New Age 2012 and beyond, crystals and stones begin to take their rightful place

CRYSTAL EMPOWERMENT BAND

Three small activated quartz crystals are needed to complete the frequency circuit for an Empowerment Band. You have a variety of choices to make the actual 'band' – some elaborate and some fairly simple. I offer here some collaborative thoughts on creating your own Empowerment Band. I hope what I offer gives you impetus to create your own!

Elastic Tape Band

You'll need 1" elastic tape, available at notions counters. Sew two lengths of elastic tape together on one edge for the size of your head. Sew 2 diagonal lines that coincide with placement forward and above your ears and 2 diagonal line that coincide with placement at the Tisra T'il (third eye chakra) forming pockets in the elastic tape. Place activated crystals in each pocket. Place band on head with one crystal placed over Tisra T'il and one on either side of head, forward of your ears.

Kerchief Band

Use a neckerchief, kerchief or large square of material. Fold it over several times to make a headband. Some folks call them 'dew rags' to catch sweat from dripping into your eyes on a hot day. You may place your crystals into the folds of the headband and position them as explained above: one over the Third Eye, and one each along side of the head, forward of your ears close to the temples.

Copper Band

For added empowerment, you can use 'dead soft' copper wire. Cut a length approximately 24 inches long. Place one crystal in the center and tightly wrap the crystal with the wire. Twist the wire to hold crystal in position. Next, measure enough wire from the center so that each of the next two crystals are positioned forward of your ears, at the temples. Wrap the wire securely around each crystal and twist the wire to hold the position. Next, place wire around your head and twist ends so headband fits comfortably. Clip off any excess wire.

An Empowerment Band can be used during meditation, contemplation, when giving Reiki or other energy healing to self and others, to receive healing energy from the side crystals and direct it with the third eye crystal back to the universe, and so on. This is a very powerful tool for balancing and healing.

Also, Empowerment Bands can be worn during toning and energy amplification to raise your vibration and energy frequency.

Each and every 'thing' on Planet Earth has its own vibration and frequency rate – people, pets, wildlife, insects, birds, fish, plants, trees, soil, rocks, stones, crystals, grains of sand, seashells, coral, driftwood, petrified wood – if it exists on Mother Earth, it vibrates at its own frequency rate. The Empowerment Band may be used to help you tune in to the different frequencies of fellow Earth Beings, animate and inanimate.

ORGONE

Orgone became a recognized energy source in the 1930s and is created by use of quartz crystal, copper, and metal shavings set in a resin base. You can create your own 'orgone buster' or 'orgone generator' as small as a pendant or as large as a bucket, depending upon need.

But, why would anyone 'want' to create an orgone generator ?

Because orgone energy is mysteriously healing and cleansing.

Orgone energy synchronizes with your personal bio-rhythm and repulses negative energy from your spirit and physical body.

It is also believed that orgone energy creates a grid of protection around an area that repulses germs, virus and bad bacteria.

Wilhelm Reich's research in the 1930s and 1940s showed that orgone energy directed at a tumor actually shrunk it. Other research showed that the human aura grew and expanded outwardly when exposed to orgone energy.

The mixture of quartz crystal, metal and resin is said to transmute "DOR" - the negative polarity of orgone energy into "OR" - positive polarity orgone energy and that when orgone busters are placed near nuclear reactors, the DOR is said to be greatly reduced.

Orgone energy generators are also believed to neutralize the DOR around ELF magnetic wave towers, HAARP and Microwave cell phone towers, alien reptilian portals, and satanic ritual sites.

There has been a lot of talk about orgone on the net, much of it skeptical, to say the least. I have had my own personal experience with orgone energy and believe that it works to some degree. First of all, dolphins seem to love orgone energy and are attracted to it.

I have simply wrapped crystals with copper and nickel wire and tossed them into the sea as a gift and blessing, only to be rewarded with a pod of dolphin swimming by! I understand that dolphin like to play with orgone balls or 'pucks' and that individual research has shown where orgone balls or pucks thrown into the water attracted dolphin. So, it was concluded that perhaps the orgone had cleaned up the water enough to sustain dolphin; they will not frequent polluted water.

This may not seem like proof positive, yet … it does make a point for the healing, clearing and cleansing energies of crystals, when mixed with copper and metals ~~ orgone energy ! The resin is simply to hold the mixture together, although it is believed that the resin creates an inert pressure upon the crystals, releasing their piezoelectric energy.

Here is a recipe for making your own orgone:

Ingredients: copper or metal mesh scrubby; copper wire; clear crystal; and resin mixture. You will also need molds. You can use plastic cups, rubber balls cut in half, bottle caps, cupcake pans or other containers to be used as a mold.

Mix the resin according to directions. Best to do this outside or in a well-ventilated area because of the resin fumes.

Coil a section of copper wire clockwise around the base of the container. Place a crystal in the center the container. Add additional pieces of copper and metal – pennies, copper or metal scrubby cut up, metal shavings, aluminum shavings, tiny aluminum foil balls. How much additional pieces of copper and metal you add depends upon the size of the container mold. Add resin to cover. Let dry for at least 12 hours, and then remove from mold. Let cure for a day or so. Your orgone is now ready to use.

What To Do With Orgone

You can make a small orgone 'buster' to carry with you for personal protection.

You can take larger orgone pucks or balls and throw them out to sea where protection and healing is needed. Dolphins have been known to pick up orgone blaster balls and carry them to where they were most needed.

You can plant orgone pucks or cup cakes around the outside of your home.

Plant them in your garden.

Place one or two near your computer, your television, any electronic equipment to offset the harming electro-magnetic fields.

Put one in your car.

Make a key chain out of a small one.

Make a small pendant using a bottle cap as a form or mold and wear it on a leather thong around your neck. Cheaper than some of the EMF protectors available online, and … perhaps holds a lot more meaning since you make it yourself with love!

Give some away as gifts for friends and family.

Where can you buy an orgone generator?

I have seen orgone generators online, in metaphysical shops, and even in a gift shop at a dinosaur dig in the Midwest! Orgone generators are available in all different shapes and sizes, and colors, as well. Some of the commercially produced orgone generators are true works of art.

CREATING AN ETHERIC STONE

As we move closer and further into the New Age, crystals, rocks and stones take their place in the physical with a direct link up to their spiritual counterparts in the higher realms. We may access the power and energy of crystals, rocks and stones etherically through use of visualization and imagination; the usage is limitless.

The word 'etheric' means "of the ether" or the mystical intangible. Creating an etheric stone simply means that we use our higher senses to imagine a crystal, rock or stone in complete detail. Once we see the stone in our mind and heart, and feel the stone with our higher senses, we create it and it becomes as real and as powerful as a tangible stone.

When we work with tangible crystals, rocks and stone, we place the stone on a part of the body, then visualize its power and send it to heal where it is needed. Etheric crystals, rocks and stones work the same way, except we create the stone and transport it telepathically.

This means that a crystal practitioner can place stones etherically via distance to heal, soothe and ease the stress of illness and dis-ease. The way it has been explained to me is that once an etheric stone has been visually created and transported to another, it remains where it is placed in full power until it is instructed to disappear.

Etheric crystals may also be used to raise the vibration or frequency of a part of the physical or spiritual body and in this way, effect healing. We can create these healing tools for ourselves or for others with their permission.

Think of the most beautiful crystal you have ever seen. See its pure water clarity, imagine each crisp and perfect angle forming a termination, look deeply into each triangular face and feel the power of the energies emanating from within it. By seeing this crystal with your imagination, you have created a perfect etheric stone.

Now that you have created this healing etheric stone, you may use it to heal or help you. Perhaps you have been suffering from a backache, or a head ache; or maybe you suffer from anxieties or fear. You can now place this etheric crystal any where you feel pain – either physically, emotionally or psychically. Using visualization, see the crystal being placed within you. Instruct this crystal to remain activated for a period of 3 hours, after which it will disappear into the unending well of Universal Life Force energy, until needed again.

You may use this book to help you create ethereal crystals, rocks and stones by looking through the stones directory, crystal directory or symptoms and issues list. Once you uncover what stone or crystal resonates for the ailment or issue you are experiencing, then you can take it into meditation to create it. For systemic maladies, you can create a gem water or gemstone elixir using etheric stones. After you create your stone, place it in drinking water, or in a small amount of brandy for an elixir. You can take the elixir by drop throughout the day for relief.

Ethereal crystals abide the spiritual Law of Economy that urges all energies to follow the path of least resistance. In order to fulfill its highest purpose, the etheric crystal or stone should be utilized to its best advantage in order to get the most out of its presence. Each stone or crystal will be affected by the power of your pure intent.

To attune yourself to a specific crystal visualize the crystal in your mind and ask it to give you all the necessary energies

Etheric stones are powerfully healing tools and there are Atlantean trained practitioners here with us today who have mastered the art of healing with etheric stones. Besides using these tools in person, these healers can send powerful elixirs, gem waters and stones via distance using Reiki or other energy medium.

CREATING AN ANGEL STONE

Every stone contains a spark of the Creator, just as we do, and hold consciousness, as well. To tap into the Angelic energies of a crystal or stone, first establish a connection with it by breathing your greeting and gratitude over it.

Any stone or crystal can become an Angel stone - it is your choice. Stones that are most receptive to Angelic presence are quartz crystal, lace agate, apophylite, moonstone, opal, fulgurite, angel aura crystals, and river rock among many other stones.

First establish what it is that you wish to convey with your Angel stone. Understand that your purpose is important so that your Angel stone knows how best to serve your needs.

The Archangels are always willing to help us achieve our goals and reach our highest purpose here on Earth. To create your angel stone use the below guide to help you..

Archangel Gabriel loves to help writers, teachers, journalists – those whose life purpose involve communication with others. Gabriel is the messenger; ask Archangel Gabriel for help in this area.

Archangel Michael is the truth speaker, whose direct manner is refreshing and sincere. Michael will help those who need courage, those who need to find their way spiritually or those who need guidance with their life's purpose. Ask, and Michael will be there for you.

Archangel Raphael is the chief healing angel, and so is the patron of healers across the universes. Doctors, nurses, therapists, light workers, energy works, Reiki healers all will benefit from Raphael's energies and love.

Archangel Uriel is the angel of illumination who helps us to clear up problems that appear to be insurmountable. Uriel will light your way if you just ask.

Archangel Zadkiel is the patron of those who wish to learn and educate themselves. If you are taking classes, wish to learn something new, or have difficulty with absorbing new knowledge, connect with Zadkiel.

Archangel Sandalphon is the patron of musicians. Connect with Sandalphon if you need inspiration.

Archangel Metatron is the patron of activity and watches over active children as well as adults. Connect with Metatron for high energy.

Archangel Jophiel is the patron of creative folks and artisans who appreciate beauty and grace.

Archangel Azrael is the patron of comfort who assists those who suffer from loss, illness, and grief. Connect with Azrael in times of trouble.

Archangel Ariel is the patron of pets, animals, plants and nature.

Archangel Chamuel is the patron of lost items.

Archangel Haniel is the patron of grace and confidence.

Once you have chosen your intent, hold your crystal or stone in your hand and lift it up to your mouth. Breathe these or similar words into your stone: "I invite you, Archangel (name), to project your protective essence here within this stone to offer your loving guidance to me. I give you my permission to enter my space and welcome you with pure intent."

If you are an artist, you might say "I love to use my creative energies to please others and ask your energies to bless this crystal."

If you are a writer, you might say "I enjoy writing and expressing myself for the benefit of others and ask your help with communicating what is in my heart through this crystal."

If you are a Reiki Practitioner, you might say .. "I enjoy using my energies for the sake of soothing and healing others and ask your help through the use of this crystal."

If you need a way of making money to pay your bills and feed your family, you might say .. "I am doing the best I can to stay on top of my financial picture and ask for your organizational and manifestation energies to lead me where I need to be to create wealth through the use of this crystal."

If you want to create a harmony angel stone, you might say "I want to create harmony, peace and balance in my relations with others and ask for your guidance through the use of this crystal."

CREATING A CRYSTAL OF LIFE

In the movie "Contact," there were stargates created that could propel us through the dimensions, more or less. What the stargate did was access the energy and power of the Flower of Life, the symbol of sacred geometry that contains the ancient wisdom of creation. The Flower of Life symbol has been recognized as far back as ancient Egypt at the Temple of Osiris and has been found all over the world in temples, palaces, cathedrals and shrines.

To create a Crystal of Life, we first make the Flower of Life Symbol by drawing a series of circles within a circle. You will need a protractor to make the circles evenly and can have fun creating your own Flower of Life. However, you may also find graphics of the Flower of Life online or in books, magazines and so forth, if you are not feeling too particularly creative.

Choose a crystal that resonates with you and place it in the center of the Flower of Life. Hold your hands over the crystal in the center of the Flower of Life and call upon the energies of the Universe to empower the crystal.

You might say ... "I ask the Universal Life Force energies to empower this crystal with love, harmony, purity and positive energy so that this Crystal of Life may be used to help me reach my highest purpose for the good of the whole in service to the All That Is."

After you have stated your petition to create a Crystal of Life, leave the crystal within the circle of the Flower of Life overnight, and meditate about your petition for the Crystal of Life before you go to sleep. When you wake up in the morning, pick up the Crystal of Life and breathe your greeting into it. You might say... "Greetings Circle of Life Crystal, it is my intent to keep you with me from this day forward for protection, assistance, and empowerment to help me reach my highest purpose in this lifetime for the good of the whole in service to the All That Is, and for this, I thank you."

If you are creating a Crystal of Life for someone else, you might say ... "I ask the Universal Life Force energies to empower this crystal with love, harmony, purity and positive energy so that this Crystal of Life may be used to help (name of recipient) to reach their highest purpose for the good of the whole in service to the All That Is."

Follow the same procedure above, that is, place the Crystal of Life within the Flower of Life circle, take the petition into meditation before going to sleep, and allow your guides to work with you during dream time to empower the crystal. When you wake up, continue the process as outlined above.

You might say ... "Greetings Circle of Life Crystal, it is my intent to give you to (name of recipient) to protect them, offer them assistance and empower them to reach their highest purpose in this lifetime for the good of the whole and in service to the All That is, and for this I am grateful."

The Circle of Life Crystal is an empowering tool that calls upon the Universal Life Force energies to bring us further along on our ascension path. You can empower any rock, stone or crystal as a Crystal of Life empowering stone through your positive energy, pure intent and love. Circle of Life crystals make wonderful birthday gifts or welcome gifts for new babies and children. They can be attached to clothing, sewn into heart-shaped pillows, or included into medicine bags. You can make them into jewelry, or use them in headbands. Ask ... and follow the energy flow you receive from your angels and guides.

CREATING CRYSTAL GRIDS

Crystal Grids are used to empower an area, large or small. You can create a blessed and sacred space by forming a crystalline grid in different alignments. These grids will protect your home, your work space, your cooking space, your car, your bathing area. You can create a temporary grid space for an occasion or purpose, or a permanent grid space, for instance to protect your home or property.

When using grids to bless and energize food that is consumed in public, you may use 'Etheric Crystals' .. *see Chapter 'Creating An Etheric Stone'.*

All grids are made with crystals and/or stones. Any stones can be used as long as you program them with your intent. I've engaged stones as small as pea gravel to facilitate a protective grid and infused them with Reiki energy while breathing my intent into their Being – I trust that the Earth gives us what we need when we need it. However, for the sake of continuity, we will be using quartz crystals in this lesson.

Grid to Empower Water and Food for Nourishment

One Crystal Grid:

For water and food, you may use the energies of one crystal. To energize a glass of water, breathe your intent over a crystal – you may use this invocation:

"I invoke the Light and power within you, Crystal, to empower and energize this water to heal and nourish me - body and soul. And, So It Is."

Drop the crystal into the vessel of water, wait one minute, then drink --- do NOT swallow the crystal. In the alternative, you may place the crystal next to the vessel of water and use the same invocation. Use discernment – if the crystal is small and there is danger of swallowing it, do not place it in the vessel. You may also strain the water using a nylon strainer to retrieve the crystal, before drinking the water.

Triangular Grid:

The Triangle calls into being two rays of power emanating from the central source forming a solid base foundation and creating a powerful connection between three points. The energies created move in continuous flow once empowered by a petition or invocation utilizing the power of three.

This grid utilizes three crystals. Place the vessel of water or container/plate of food on a flat surface. Create a grid by placing three crystals around the food. One at the top, the second at the lower right and the third crystal at the lower left, surrounding the food within the triangular grid. As you place each crystal, breathe this invocation over the crystal:

"I invoke the Light and Power within you, Crystal, to empower and energize this food to heal and nourish me body and soul. This space will continue to emanate power for three minutes. And, So It Is."

Allow the crystalline grid to work for three minutes before consuming your food.

Square Grid:

The square signifies balance and equality. It calls upon the four compass points – north, south, east and west - to energize harmony and parity within the space it creates.

Utilizing four crystals, place vessel of water or container of food on flat surface. Create grid by forming a square with crystals around the water or food.

"I invoke the Light and Power within you, Crystal, to empower and energize this food to heal and nourish me body and soul. This space will continue to emanate power for four minutes. And, So It Is."

You may use the Square Grid for larger portions of food and water and also for large gatherings where balance and harmony are desirous.

Grid Around Your Home:

Place a crystal at every right corner angle around the outside of the home . For apartments, you can place a crystal in the outside corner inside the apartment.

Use this invocation as you place each crystal:

"I invoke the Light and Power within you, Crystal, to protect this structure with Love, Light and Harmony. This space will continue to emanate power until directed otherwise by me. And, So It Is."

Grid around your water bath, shower or swimming pool

You may use either a triangle or square grid around the outside of the bathtub. For modern tubs where there are ledges around the inside of the tub, you may place one crystal in each corner forming a square grid. For older tubs, you may place the crystals outside of the tub to form a grid.

For swimming pools – use a square grid for rectangular pools, one crystal in each corner. For round pools, use a triangular grid .

Crystal Placement

For round pools, place the east crystal first, north second and south third. For square pools, use the same configuration but add west crystal placement last. This grid makes advantageous use of the healing energies of the sun as it rises and sets to protect the swimming area within the pool and to disseminate healing energies to all those who swim there.

Grid for a Vehicle

You may make a one-crystal grid inside your vehicle by suspending a crystal inside the vehicle. Crystal pendulums work very well in this case because they are already attached to a chain. Crystal necklaces also work well. Loose crystals are not a good idea because they could become projectiles too easily. Always secure your crystal(s) in your vehicle.

Invocation

"I invoke the Light and Power within you, Crystal, to protect this vehicle and those who ride within it with Love, Light, safety and security. This space will continue to emanate power until directed otherwise by me. And, So It Is."

I have used crystals in a velveteen pouch placed inside the console of my car, programmed them for protection, and there they remain today, available to me when I need them, and out of the way for safety purposes.

Circular "Wheel" Grid

My sister Nancy Becker, a Reiki Master and Teacher, uses this grid to keep her loved ones close in her heart and positive energy sessions. It is a beautiful way to visually send healing energy to those you love and those who request it.

She uses a small round accent table with a removable glass top. Under the glass she places people's names hand written on slips of paper and/or their photos. On top of the glass, she creates a power grid using quartz crystals. She sends Reiki energy to the grid to empower it and effect healing to those listed. This is a very powerful tool to manifest desires, as well.

CRYSTAL DEPOSITS IN THE US

It has been said that the closer to the earth's core crystal formations lie, the stronger their magnetic field. This has been proven scientifically. There are a number of areas around the planet where the conditions are perfect for the creation of quartz crystals. Here in the United States, Central-West and North-West Arkansas is home to the largest mine field for quartz crystal. And because this mine field is closely connected to the Earth's core, Arkansas provides some of the best transmitter crystals in the world. Arkansas crystals are the purest form of crystals in the world and they emit very powerful electromagnetic energies.

There are smaller pockets of crystals in Georgia, North Carolina, Arizona, California and Nevada in the United States. New York State has the singular distinction of having its own water clear crystal that lies near anthracite veins in the Herkimer County area, aptly named Herkimer Diamonds. Herkimer Diamonds are not actually diamonds, but rather a clear quartz, some with anthracite inclusions. However, interestingly enough, Arkansas, the crystal capital of the world, lies approximately 30 miles north of the Crater of Diamonds in Murfreesboro, Arkansas, which is home to the only open-to-the-public diamond bearing site.

Brazil is also well known for its crystal mines in the north east section around Diamantina. Also very powerful crystals can be found in Minas Gerais, Brazil where the Super Seven Stone was discovered. Elsewhere in Tibet, Madagascar and Siberia, among other areas.

On a recent trip to Arkansas, we visited three different crystal mines, chatted with a number of store keepers and discovered that crystal mining is more than just a popular tourist attraction. It seems that mining gets 'in the blood' and miners are very serious about what they do, how they do it and why. Here is some information on the mines that we visited:

Bear Mountain Crystal Mine – located on top of Fiddler's Ridge about 7 miles south of Mt. Ida. Did not appear to be an active mine, but is definitely not depleted. Primitive location, difficult to find. We discovered some absolutely beautiful clear crystals there, including some beautiful but small clear clusters. There is an incredibly gorgeous 360 degree mountain view, but no comfort facilities so it is best to come prepared for nature calls in the wild. You will work hard, but it is worth a visit. You will be on your own here. We were told that this mine was picked over – but I don't believe it because we found a lot of nice pieces here. It was work, but definitely well worth it.

The approach to Bear Mountain Mine is flat out scary. There are no signs, so we had to zero our trip meter and travel exactly 1.6 miles to an old rock that was painted silver .. 'was' painted silver .. it had faded quite a bit! We turned into a narrow dirt path and traveled for a bit .. maybe a half-mile into the woods up a steep incline. There were no turn around spots carved into the woods, so you either went straight up the mountain or you backed down the mountain. It was raining, wet and the road was rocky; some parts of it were down-right treacherous.

There was no signage identifying the mine at the gate. The gate was a very heavy pipe that extended across the road anchored to two pipes sunk into the ground. I hoisted the pipe up on my shoulder and walked the gate open. Once open, we continued up the very steep and very wet rocky road to the mine.

When we got to the top, we were completely awed ~~ what a view !! Before we started to look around for a place to start, we stopped to contemplate the beauty of the area. Mountaintop after mountaintop rolled away into the distance no matter which way you looked. Brownie points for awesome, raw beauty!

Words of caution. There are no facilities at Bear Mountain Mine, so be prepared for emergencies. Take food and water with you because the mine is about 10 miles or so from town and .. the road into the mine can be dangerous, not one you would want to drive up and down numerous times quickly.

We did not have 4WD and were able to access the mine without too much difficulty, but 4WD is recommended. It is on 'top' of the mountain as are all the crystal mines –the crystal veins run along the crest of the mountains – so remember that you will be going up some steep inclines. The road to Bear Mountain Mine can best be described as primitive at the time we visited.

Once you are there, be prepared to stay until you are finished digging. Also, be prepared to take out what you take in, meaning, water bottles, plastic bags and so forth; there are no trash receptacles at the mine. You know how the saying goes … "Leave no trace."

We stayed till after 4 pm, rain or not, and had a dandy of a time sloshing in the mud, climbing up and down the tailings piles. We never saw a snake or bug – just a lot of 'daddy long leg' spiders who kept leading us to crystals ! We found some lovely clusters, small, clear and bright, at Bear Mountain. It did not, however, appear to be an active mine when we visited. The equipment is there, but no body was there operating it. We were told in town that they hadn't been doing a lot of digging up there ~~ but learned a valuable lesson, don't believe everything you hear. We were very pleased with what we found! And, I've recently learned that they are back digging and mining again with some wonderful finds.

Bottom Line: Add Bear Mountain Mine at Fiddler's Ridge to your itinerary. If you plan on visiting a few crystal mines, save this one for last because there may not be anyone around to show you what to do, or how to identify what you are looking for. However, it is definitely worth the trip. Many of the small, clear crystals that we found were from here. The road leading to the mine is very poor, the mine owner pretty much leaves you alone and you really have to dig for your finds ~~ but it is really, really fun. This is NOT a seeded dig site.

Gee & Dee Crystal Mine – located just outside of Story, AR 13 miles north of Mt. Ida. Gee & Dee Mine was good for fun, though we never saw the actual mine. We were taken to a 'special dig site' which we feel may have been seeded with clear crystals because we did find a few; we also found leaf mold 6 to 8 inches under the soil -- unusual. Our findings were mostly white quartz rock. Great place for a fun dig, not for the serious digger at this 'special dig site' though. Wished we did see the real mine because we heard this was a great spot to find clear quartz.

We were greeted by co-owner, Dee Johnson who is quite an accomplished woman in her own right. Besides being co-owner of an active crystal mine, she is also an archeologist and genuine knowledgeable person. Ms. Dee was very helpful, and got right in the trenches with us – literally – to show us how to dig, where to dig and what to look for.

The Gee & Dee site where we were digging was not like any of the other mines we had visited. There was no visible track-hoe or dozer equipment. It was on a very steep hillside, rather than tailings piles. The site appeared to have been backfilled and had a one year growth of pine seedlings. We were instructed to dig amongst the roots and 10 foot area forward of the pine seedlings as a 'special' dig site. We were not taken to the crystal mine. Nevertheless, we truly had fun and Ms. Dee offered us a discounted "Senior Citizen" rate to dig! Can't balk at that!

On a good note, Gee & Dee Crystal Mine offered comfort facilities, primitive as it may have been – when ya gotta go, ya gotta go ! And Ms. Dee was very generous offering us coffee and chips and other edibles. She is truly a lovely woman with a huge heart! I'd love to see the real mine on our next trip !

Words of Caution: The road to the mine, although very good and accessible, is also very long and winding. We must have gone in and up about 2 miles via switchback before we found the dig site at the top of the mountain. Again, because of the location and distance from town, be prepared with your own water and food. We were fortunate that it was an overcast day; even still, we got very thirsty and can't imagine how hot it must be when the sun is blazing. Take lots of water or drinks with you to stay replenished.

My suggestion ~~ go here for fun. If you do take the kids, be careful if you are going to this particular dig site at Gee & Dee Mine because the drop off below is about 20 feet .

Sweet Surrender Crystal Mine – located outside of Story, AR, 10 miles north of Mt. Ida. Absolutely the best – best location, best crystals, best and most helpful mine owners. Randy Skates and Becky Young are lovely folks who are very serious about their business. And they should be because they have absolutely gorgeous clear quartz crystals – everywhere. We were greeted, helped, and just became enthralled with Sweet Surrender – the energies are fantastic.

Hands down, Sweet Surrender Crystal Mine is the best place to dig crystals … and for many reasons. First is crystal quality. Second, the owners, Randy Skates and Becky Young are fantastic folks – helpful, knowledgeable and just plain good people. Third, the road to get there is very good. Fourth, their lay out is very user friendly – picnic table, benches, trash can. However, no restroom facilities are available, so … be prepared, in case! Becky is the greatest in showing you what to look for, pointing out crystals to you, and helping you to understand what you are doing. Plus she is an incredibly gifted and talented woman in her own right. Randy has been crystal mining for over 30 years and he knows his stuff inside out and upside down; just hearing him speak so lovingly of these wonderful treasures is a learning experience in itself.

Randy explains that his mine is in alignment with a very large crystal deposit that travels 17 miles northward. We can attest to this as fact since … we dug some gorgeous specimens from Sweet Surrender Crystal Mine.

The landscape is very easy to navigate. We visited Sweet Surrender on a Friday, and they had just excavated on Wednesday, so .. the tailings piles we were digging in were not picked over and crystals just stood there and looked at us all pretty-like !

Bottom Line: Definitely go to Sweet Surrender Crystal Mine – if you only visit one mine, let this one be it. It is easy access, the owners are lovely people, and the mine is nowhere near depleted, even though Randy admits that over a million dollars worth of crystal has come out of the mine so far --- it ain't over till the fat lady sings, and I don't even hear her tuning up! The crystals we found were mostly clear or part clear/part clouded; very little opaque quartz. Be prepared to work with acid in the cleaning process; these crystals can be heavily coated with iron oxide. Detailed cleaning instructions can be found at end of this section.

The Crystal Seen Trading Co. is also a definite stop if you visit Mt. Ida. It is located right on Hwy 270 and the owners, Julie and Dennis Kincaid are like a breath of fresh air – truly delightful folks and very knowledgeable. The Crystal Seen is the only metaphysical shop in Mt. Ida at the time of this writing and is a great experience- They have crystals, stones, jewelry and lots of love in their shop. Also have a small mine, plus a seeded dig site for fun. We didn't try our luck, but … wished we had. Next trip, for sure!

Jay's Bonanza on Hwy 270 in Mt. Ida is another good stop. Plenty of crystals and stones for sale, and the folks there are really nice people, very helpful and offered us a lot of information.

Words of Note About The Mt. Ida Mines: There are quite a few crystal mines in and around Mt. Ida, Arkansas. Depending upon where you live, it could be a long drive and an expensive trip.

While the accommodations are not expensive and although the area is quite beautiful, gas, food and lodging does mount up. At $20 a day to dig at the mines, it is still a fun and exciting trip, but don't get your hopes up for that 'one, big piece" of crystal that will make you rich.

Out of all the digging we did at all three of the mines we visited, we ended up with maybe 2 pounds of clear quartz crystal each, not counting some of the large clusters we dug up that were embedded in sandstone chert.

Our best get were two bushel baskets of crystals that we purchased wholesale from Randy Skates of Sweet Surrender Crystal Mines – One bushel contained three huge clusters that were loaded with clear quartz crystals. The other bushel contained about 40 pounds of small clusters and clear crystal points.

Accommodations: Choose carefully. We stayed at the Ozark Cabin which is associated with Fiddler's Ridge Rock Shop and Bear Mountain Crystal Mine. The cabin was lovely, quiet, clean and comfortable. It was also affordable. At the time of our visit, there was no WiFi. However, there is WiFi at the library in town so we spent some time in the parking lot catching up with email and so forth.

Maureen Walther of the Mt. Ida Chamber of Commerce told us that the Royal Oak Inn has WiFi … we highly recommend that you check with her before you make reservations. Maureen is fantastic and extremely helpful. She will guide you to what you need. There are cabins on the lake (Lake Ouachita is 'right there' .. and beautiful), RV sites, three motels that we saw and numerous bed and breakfasts in the area. Visit the Mt. Ida Chamber of Commerce web site for great info on where to stay, as well as what to do, and where to do it !

Another good note .. we had excellent cellular service in Mt. Ida using Verizon. Evidently, Mt. Ida used to be an Alltel cell area and now is incorporated into the Verizon network. Our Alltel phone worked great!

Places to Eat: Three places in Mt. Ida itself – the Mt. Ida Café, the El Diamante Mexican Restaurant and the Dairyette. We opted for the Mt. Ida Café for breakfast and dinner and everything was excellent – service, food and great coffee !

The El Diamante restaurant looked busy and popular, but we didn't try it. We did, however, stop by the Dairyette for yummy ice cream; they also serve burgers and fast food goodies.

~

SEMI PRECIOUS AND PRECIOUS GEM LOCATIONS WORLDWIDE

No matter where you live on Planet Earth, you are 'thisclose' to a gem mining region, whether semi-precious or precious. From Thunder Bay, Ontario in Canada, to Bisbee, Arizona, from Afghanistan to Australia, gemstones are mined in earnest. And there are many places where you can go dig your own, or at least, have a go at the tailings piles. I suggest that you contact the Chamber of Commerce in the area where you would like to 'rock hound' and hopefully the following information will whet your appetite a bit.

Although I'm not suggesting you visit these spots to hand-dig your rocks and stones, it is interesting to see just how far some stones have to travel before they find their place around your finger or neck.

Afghanistan is known as a repository for aquamarine, emerald, garnet, kunzite, lapis lazuli, ruby, sapphire, tourmaline, turquoise and zircon.

India is also a large repository for garnet, emerald, amethyst, and aquamarine.

Many colored gemstones are found in Sri Lanka, Asia and Brazil, South America. However, Africa is today generating an enormous amount of activity. Diamonds have been mined in Africa, particularly in the southern and eastern regions from Namibia, Zimbabwe, Mozambique, Malawi and Tanzania. Active areas are found in Kenya, Madagascar and outer islands.

Colored gemstones from Africa are ruby, sapphire, tourmaline, aquamarine, chrysoberyl, andalusite, apatite, citrine, iolite, and kyanite. Tanzanite, spinel, thodolite and tsavorite garnets are also found here.

Nigeria is one of the largest sources of blue sapphire and tourmaline, as well as pyrope and almandine garnet, aquamarine and topaz.

Canada is one of the largest sources of diamonds in North America and also produces a multitude of stones including amethyst, beryl, emerald, agate, garnet, jasper, calcite, celestine, diopside, epidote, amazonite among many other semi and precious gems and minerals. Digging and rock hounding can be done in almost any of the provinces including diamonds and amethysts in Ontario.

In the United States, gems stones and precious minerals can be found in every State and there are many places where you can go dig your own, pan the streams, pour through a sluice or scour the tailings piles.

Gold, peridot, turquoise, silver, petrified wood, malachite, garnet, peridot, agate, jasper, opal and many other wonderful stones can be found in Arizona.

Nevada is known for turquoise and opal.

California is well known for tourmaline, turquoise and gold. You could also find diamond, chrysoprase, jadeite, jasper, petrified wood and quartz in California.

Oregon is known for feldspar, sunstone, red labradorite, agates, jaspers and obsidian.

Besides lava stone, you can also find petrified wood, and agate in Washington State. Its shoreline produces pearl.

Wyoming is an excellent spot for agate, jade, bloodstone, sapphire and rubies. You can also find diamonds, opal, peridot, iolite, petrified wood and quartz in Wyoming.

Idaho produces garnet, opal, agate, sapphire and obsidian.

Montana holds some of the most beautiful deposits of sapphire, garnet, topaz, gold and ruby with quite a few mines open to the public.

Utah is known for topaz, garnet, petrified wood, moqui marbles, jasper and obsidian.

You'll find Black Hills Gold in South Dakota, and gold in North Dakota as well, along with chalcedony, agate, petrified wood and beryl.

New Mexico is known for turquoise, garnet, peridot, crystal and obsidian.

Arkansas is not only known for its incredible water-clear quartz, but also for diamonds at the Crater of Diamonds State Park.

North Carolina on the east coast is known for its potential as a gold mining state. Also, North Carolina and South Carolina both boast emeralds, ruby, garnets, citrine, amethyst, topaz and quartz.

Georgia also has a ridge of quartz on its southeast side. Northern Georgia is good for panning gold, and finding amethysts and rutile quartz.

Alabama produces quartz, gold and blue and yellow beryl.

Mississippi is a frequent spot for pearl and also chalcedony as well as petrified wood.

Missouri is a producer of fluorite, pyrite and calcite.

Kansas is popular for Kansas pop rocks, known as Boji™ Stones, and also chalcedony.

Maine is great digging for tourmaline, beryl, rose quartz, topaz, quartz and aquamarine.

New York is known for Herkimer diamonds, beryl, brown tourmaline, garnet and rose quartz.

Pennsylvania produces amethyst, almandine and pyrope garnet, beryl, moonstone and sunstone.

No matter where you go in the United States, you can find a stone that has meaning to you, and perhaps also one that is worth passing on to your grandkids.

DIG YOUR OWN QUARTZ CRYSTALS AND STONES IN ARKANSAS

Digging for crystals is a dirty job, no other way of saying it nicely. The soil in which quartz crystals grow is mostly red clay colored by iron oxide and it stains most everything it touches. Wear old clothes, or clothing that you won't mind getting dirty.

When we went to the mines, it rained, which made for a lot of mud; however the rain also softened up the ground and washed away some of the top soil so we were able to find some beautiful crystals right on top of the ground, or exposed enough of the crystals so we could see them more easily with little effort. However, this is really hard work. The tailings piles are huge with lots of rocks and all are covered in red dirt. You've got to do a lot of climbing up and down the tailings piles and that is work in itself. So .. be prepared to climb, dig, and get dirty !

Equipment can be anything from long screwdrivers (which we preferred), to small garden claws, to hammers, mallets, crowbars, pick axes, hand rakes – anything that you can use to dig around in the muck. If you work the tailings piles, you won't need anything more than some garden tools and …. the treasured long screwdriver.

You'll need buckets – 5 gallon size is great – and for more than just to carry your findings. We only went to one mine that had comfort facilities --- read that – an outhouse, so … you might consider having a 'nature' bucket for the 'in cases'.

Also .. bring lots of water or drink and bring lunch too. The mines are not in the town of Mt. Ida. It could be a long and even treacherous drive back and forth depending on what mine you visit and whether or not it is raining. Keep in mind that the mines are on top of the mountains. Granted, these are not the Rockies, but .. nevertheless, you will have to drive some pretty steep and primitive roads to get to the top of the mountain where the crystals are

How To Dig

Most mines do not permit you to actually dig in their pit. OSHA and insurance companies eschew such an arrangement. However, mine owners using heavy equipment will dig out of the mine pit and deposit the 'tailings' into huge dirt piles. This is what you will normally encounter. And this indeed is the most fun !

I discovered something interesting … I noticed that I wasn't actually digging, I was more or less 'raking' across the dirt and then looking for a tell-tale sign of a crystal. Using hand held garden tools and an extra long screw driver were all that were needed to uncover a treasure trove of beautiful crystals.

What To Look For

Look for the glint or shine. Most crystals are disguised by red dirt, but .. after a rain, you may be able to see just a hint of glint .. dig for it ! It just may be a beautifully clear quartz crystal !

Don't be fooled by quartz rock, because there may be a lot of that too – white quartz, which is lovely as it is, but … it is not the prized clear quartz crystal and when it is covered in red clay, you'll have a hard time telling the difference.

Make good use of your garden hand tools; a claw and a hand rake are perfect for moving the soil around and uncovering the crystals. Just rake the sides of the piles in a large arc, starting from the top of your reach and raking down toward the bottom. This action helps you to cover a lot of ground quickly. If you happen to see something large in the pile, you can use the long handled screwdriver to help wedge it out, or dig around it to separate it from the pile.

You might consider bringing a spray bottle with you to remove a bit of dirt from the stone to uncover your finds!

How To Clean Your Crystals:

We were told by a lovely gal at Jay's Bonanza in the heart of Mt. Ida to take our findings to the local car wash and use the power washer on 'rinse' to blast away the dirt from the crystals and clusters we found. It worked !

However, if you have to travel any distance to get your treasures back home, you might consider keeping that protective dirt and mud around your crystals until you get home. The car wash is still a good idea to blast away that mud and dirt once you get home, and the dirt will protect your finds during the ride home.

Once we got home with all our treasures, we set out to clean what we had so we could 'triage' them to see which would get the Muriatic acid bath, which would get just the oxalic acid bath, and which we would leave intact with dirt. Using toothbrushes and dish cleaning brushes, we started to clean and remove the remaining vestiges of mud and dirt before we went to the acid bath phase. This was dirty work. The brushes sprayed muddy water droplets everywhere. We tried to hose the crystals off, but ... to get deeper into the crevices, we needed brushes.

Once we were satisfied about cleaning them off, we went to the cooker. Yep ... we cooked the crystals in an oxalic acid bath. Oxalic acid is heat activated and works great at cleaning off any lime or mineral residuals.

You'll need a way to bring the oxalic acid and water mixture to a rolling boil before letting it set to cool. I used an old electric 30 quart cooker that was set outside on the open back porch.

You can also us an outside electric or propane stove, or a wood fire, to get the acid to a rolling boil\. A stainless steel stock pot works well, but .. use one that you have no intention of ever using for food again.

Use 1 lb of oxalic acid powder to 2 ½ gallons water. We used an old 30 quart electric cooker and placed all the crystals in plastic baskets. It was easier to remove the baskets with the cleaned crystals than to dig them out of the acid with a fish net.

While the oxalic acid was doing its thing, we placed some of the very crusty rusty clusters in a plastic 5 gallon bucket. Each cluster has been washed off as best we could and we were now willing to let the muriatic acid do the rest of the work. But .. this stuff is dangerous. Do not touch it. Do not breathe the fumes. Use chemical-type plastic gloves, and stay away from smoke that comes out of the bottle when you open it. We bought muriatic acid at the hardware store in gallon jugs. It will take an hour just to read the cautions on the bottle. Don't shake it. Keep it upright. Do not get on skin. Lord … what were we getting ourselves into!

Well, it was not all that bad. With a little common sense, you can do the muriatic acid bath just fine. First we tried to use 1 pint of muriatic acid to 2 gallons of water. No effect on the iron oxide. So, we stepped it up … 2 pints. Nothing. What we ended up doing is pouring the muriatic acid straight over the crystals and letting them sit for 5 days. WOW .. that worked ! By the way, we were told to use 18% muriatic acid. The hardware store did not have 18%, it only had 33%, which is why we tried to cut it with water. Don't waste your time … just use it straight. At least, that is what we did with success.

We moved the muriatic acid into another 5 gallon bucket and then rinsed the crystals clean by flushing them with a garden hose. This was not a quick rinse; we continued to flush the crystals with fresh water by filling up the bucket a number of times. Then, we placed the crystals into the oxalic acid bath to cook. When they came out .. you would never have guessed that these crystals were so totally encrusted with iron oxide because now they were perfect .. beautiful, clear, and clean! Wow!

To deactivate the muriatic acid and the oxalic acid, use baking soda; then you can just throw it away. Otherwise .. you can keep the oxalic and muriatic to use again. Word of note: When you add the baking soda to the acid solution, step back, because as it deactivates the acid, it foams up and over the container. With the muriatic acid solution, I continued to add baking soda a little at a time until the foaming action slowed down.

Also, we found a product on the grocer's shelf that also worked for removing iron oxide from the crystals – it is called "The Works" rust remover. It is the same thing as CLR – both products are oxalic acid based and if you use them straight on the crystals and let them sit for 5 days, they will remove the iron oxide. We tried this on a few small crystals. All that was needed afterwards was a good scrub with a toothbrush and fresh water and those few crystals sparkled like glass. Amazing.

It was also suggested that we leave the muddy crystals out in the sun to bake for a while, then hose them off, set them out to dry again, then .. hose them off. Repeat the cycle until the dirt is gone. This process could take a week or so to accomplish but is a viable alternative to the car wash technique of mud removal.

Another suggestion was to place the hosed off crystals in the dishwasher and use "Finish" to clean them. At first we didn't try this method, however ... after cleaning, soaking, drying in the sun, blasting with a power washer, soaking in more acid, spraying with bleach and so on, I gave the dishwasher a try on some of the more difficult pieces. This was not a bad idea, and worked well on the larger clusters.

I also tried using a 'Water Pik" which acted like a mini-power washer and was able to get into some of the teeny crevices in between crystals on the larger clusters. This worked well.

What Do You Do With Your Crystals After Cleaning ?

Well .. as a metaphysician, and energy practitioner I use the crystals in my work. I also give them away to clients, friends and family after blessing them and working with them. Some of the hand-dug crystals have already traveled the world, some across the nation, and some stayed close to home.

Some of the larger clusters may be staying here at home. Some will be gifts. And some of the small clear points have found their way into jewelry, earrings and wire wrapped pendants. Some of the white quartz pieces now adorn my flower gardens.

What you do with them is entirely up to you.

Make a grid around your home, your room, your bed.

Arrange them in your garden with your flowers,

Place them in your house plants.

Create orgone balls for the dolphins.

Sleep with them, talk to them, bathe with them – generally, invite them into your home and make them family!

EPILOGUE

Crystals are wonderful creations. There is nothing like being the first human to actually hold a crystal for the first time in its life! That is truly an honor.

Once a crystal is birthed from the Earth, and you pick it up, you are then charged with its responsibility, to clean it, cherish it, and find it permanent place topside.

Whether you hand dig your own crystals, or purchase them in a metaphysical shop, I encourage you to explore the wisdom and energy afforded by befriending one, or ... many !

My life has become so greatly enriched by acquainting myself with crystals, rocks, stones, seashells, coral and driftwood. I know that you, too, have something to gain through this type of association.

As we step forward into the New Age, we will have the opportunity of becoming more adept at focusing on the unusual, what may have once been not so norm, takes center stage and now becomes readily acceptable. The use of rocks, crystals and stones are on the agenda for the New Age. Enjoy the power!

ABOUT THE AUTHOR

Barbara S. Delozier, Msc.D. is a metaphysical practitioner and generationally gifted spiritual counselor. She has helped thousands of people find joy and satisfaction in their lives through the use of Mother Nature's bounty ~ crystals, rocks, stones, sea shells and driftwood. While employing positive affirmations, affirmative treatments, negative reversal, and guided meditation, Barbara has encouraged others to walk their journey with trust in the process of all life.

Barbara is the founder of Greater Good Ministries, an online pastoral outreach and GGMRadio, a psychic, spiritual and metaphysical talk radio outreach which features inspirational programming and music 24 hours a day, seven days a week.

Barbara's work is featured at her portal site ~ http://Empower-U.org ~ from where you may gain entry into a very special world.

All Inspiration ...
All The Time

http://GGMRadio.com

GREATER GOOD MINISTRIES
RADIO WWW.GGMRADIO.COM

GGMRadio is available 24 hours a day, seven days a week on the internet and via Itunes ~ perfect at work, at home, anywhere you want to create a positive, inspirational atmosphere with uplifting music and talk radio programming.

Interfaith services are broadcast live every Sunday morning at 1 PM Eastern time with convenient rebroadcasts at 5 and 8 pm eastern with rotating interfaith ministers bringing uplifting messages of hope and joy.

Rev. Nancy Becker hosts *"Wake Up To A Brighter Morn,"* live every Monday at 10 am Eastern with rebroadcasts Monday through Friday at 6 am and 10 am over GGMRadio.com.

"Messages of Light" with Amanda Dowel airs at Noon Eastern every Monday, featuring special guests and Amanda's own angelic wisdom.

The *"Spice of Life Cooking Show – Home Edition"* airs every Tuesday at 11 am Eastern time with host Rosanne Bolton.

The *"Spice of Life Cooking Show – International Edition"* is hosted by Rev. Debra Wright and airs in archives with quarterly live programming.

Lydia Aswolf hosts *"Lydia's Literary Lowdown"* every Tuesday at 2 pm Eastern, featuring special guests, book reviews and finger-on-the-pulse timely topics.

Wednesdays at Noon Eastern time brings Lydia Aswolf's and Suzanne Soria's ever-popular *"Psychically Correct"* to the airwaves, alternating with a special guest one week, and full-on psychic readings the next week.

Ms. Peg Torbert starts out Thursday's line up alternating each week between *"Ms. Peg's Power Hour"* with special guests and free mini readings and *"Trinity Psychics"* with Bee, featuring topics of timely interest in the metaphysical and spiritual arena.

Tena Marie Harris hosts *"Primarily Paranormal"* at 9 pm Eastern on Thursday featuring special guests, free mini readings and assistance with matters relating to hauntings, ghosts, spirits and the nether world.

Fridays brings in *"Open Heart Teachings"* at 7 pm Eastern with a rotating host schedule of spiritual coaches who joyfully bring messages of enlightenment from Ascended Masters and high level spiritual guides.

At 9 pm Eastern, Barbara "Rev. Bee" Delozier comes on with *"Heart and Soul"* featuring timely topics, guided meditations, free mini-readings and special guests from the metaphysical field.

8:30 pm Eastern on Saturdays is the syndicated rebroadcast of *"The Edge on Utopia Radio"* with Rev. Barbara "Bee" Delozier. *"The Edge"* airs worldwide live every Tuesday at 12:30 pm Eastern time over UtopiaRadio.com.

Rounding out the GGMRadio schedule is the popular *"Life Journeys"* with host Thomas Hayden at 10 pm Eastern every Saturday featuring topics of challenge surrounding love and relationships, paranormal encounters and with free mini readings.